PLANETARY MOVEMENTS AND THEIR IMPACT ON HUMAN LIVES

Srinivasan Gopalan

Publishers
UNICORN BOOKS
F-2/16, Ansari Road, Daryaganj, New Delhi-110002
☎ Ph.: 011-23275434, 23262683, 23250704
E-mail: info@unicornbooks.in • *Website:* www.unicornbooks.in

Branch : Mumbai
23-25, Zaoba Wadi, Thakurdwar, Mumbai-400002
☎ 022-22010941, 022-22053387
E-mail: unicornbooksmumbai@gmail.com

ISBN 978-81-7806-571-7

Edition: 2021

Printed at : Param Offsetters, Okhla, New Delhi-110020

To those who keep persisting and never give up

Acknowledgement

In the age of Social Media, I thank you for finding the time and picking up this book. The idea of a book goes through multiple phases and is rarely the effort of one individual. For this book too, I have many to thank.

My family – The pillar of my life. My mother Raji Gopalan, my father R.Gopalan and my sister Swetha Gopalan. Thank you for always being there.

My friends, acquaintances and critics whose valuable feedback and critique on my previous books has motivated me to try and communicate a number of concepts which hopefully will be more suited to resolving their queries on such topics.

My publisher, Dr. Ashok Gupta and his team at Unicorn Books – Thank you for your continued support in publishing this book that deals with specific topics on planetary movements in Vedic astrology.

Last but not least, my readers – This book would not be what it is without your constant support and unwavering quest for enhanced knowledge. I hope this book goes a long way in enriching that quest.

Contents

Chapter 1

Retrograde Motion of Planets

One of the most important concepts in Vedic astrology when we talk about planetary movements is the retrograde motion of planets. The term retrogression or retrograde motion of planets simply refers to the apparent movement of the planets in the solar system in a direction that is opposite to their normal course of action. Let us examine this concept more thoroughly.

The solar system as we know consists of 9 planets, namely Mercury, Venus, Earth, Mars, Jupiter, Saturn, Uranus, Neptune and Pluto. While Mercury and Venus are known as the "Inner Planets", the planets Mars to Pluto are termed as the "Outer Planets" (In this book we will restrict the discussion on outer planets to Mars, Jupiter and Saturn).

We also know that the 9 planets of the solar system rotate about their own axis and revolve around the Sun in an elliptical orbit in an "eastward" direction. Motions in this direction are referred to as *direct* motions. There are however periods when the planets appear to recede or move in an opposite direction than what is normal for them. Motions in this direction are referred to as *retrograde* motions.

Astronomically speaking, when a planet goes from *perihelion* (the part of a planet's orbit nearest to the Sun) to aphelion (the part of a planet's orbit most distant from the Sun) as it recedes from the Sun, it gradually loses the power of the Sun's gravitation and consequently to gain it, it retrogrades (This would indicate that planets in retrograde motion move at a faster pace than when they are in direct motion). Likewise, when the planet comes from aphelion to perihelion, the gravitational pull of the Sun results in the planet starting to accelerate, making it appear move in a direct manner for an observer on earth.

Retrograde Motion in Vedic Astrology:

Vedic astrology is based on the principles of the planetary motion of the navagrahas (Sun, Moon, Mars, Mercury, Jupiter, Venus, Saturn, Rahu and Ketu) through the 12 zodiac signs or rashis. In normal course of action, the 9 planets traverse clockwise from Mesha (Aries) rashi to Meena (Pisces) rashi. For example, once Jupiter transits Makara rashi, it will then move onto Kumbha rashi. This is the normal or direct motion of the planet.

Among the navagrahas, the Sun and the Moon are always direct in motion and can never be retrograde. Sun will always transit from Vrishabha rashi to Mithuna rashi. Think about the fact that in the Gregorian calendar the month of June follows May and not the other way around. In a similar manner, Ashalesha nakshatra always precedes Magha nakshatra. Thus, the Moon will always move from Kataka rashi to Simha rashi.

The 2 mathematical nodes of the Moon, Rahu and Ketu which are also known as illusionary planets or *chaya grahas* are the exact opposite. They move in a retrograde or anticlockwise manner through the 12 rashis. So, once Rahu has transited Vrischika rashi, it will move to Tula rashi and not Dhanu rashi as is the convention.

The remaining 5 planets known as *tara grahas* (Mars, Jupiter, Saturn, Mercury, Venus) are generally direct in motion but will periodically turn retrograde from time to time.

In Vedic astrology, retrograde motion is defined as the apparent backward motion of a planet caused by it being lapped by another planet. We all know that different planets in the solar system have different orbital periods around the Sun. If we take any pair of two planets in the solar system, we will notice that both the planets appear to move in a direct motion around the Sun but the planet with the smaller orbit moves faster than the planet with the larger orbit and when it passes the slower moving planet, each sees the other one as apparently moving backwards relative to its usual motion around the sky.

The 3 outer planets of Mars, Jupiter and Saturn have longer orbital periods when compared to Earth. As a result, the Earth passes by or overtakes the outer planets periodically, which cause the outer planets to appear to move backwards for an observer on planet Earth. Likewise, the two inner planets of Mercury and Venus have smaller orbital periods when compared to Earth and when they lap Earth, they appear to be moving backwards.

In reality the planet concerned is not moving backward but there is a difference in relative motion of the planet w.r.t Earth which causes it to appear as being in retrograde motion. Think about 2 cars "A" and "B" traveling at 60 KMPH on a highway and suddenly "A" accelerates and starts traveling at 90 KMPH. It will appear to "A" that "B" is moving backwards although in reality "B" is moving forward albeit at a speed slower when compared to "A".

This concept of retrograde motion is not applicable to the Sun and the Moon in Vedic astrology. The earth constantly revolves around the Sun while the Moon orbits the Earth. Retrograde motion in Vedic astrology comes into play when two pairs of planets orbit a third planet or a celestial object (eg: Earth and Mars orbiting the Sun).

On the other hand, Rahu and Ketu, the two nodes of the Moon's orbit, move in sync with each other due to the action of Sun's gravity on the Moon's motion in an anticlockwise manner. Thus, their normal motion is always retrograde.

We have thus established that in Vedic astrology, among the 9 planets, the **Sun and Moon are always direct in motion, Rahu and Ketu are always retrograde** while **Mars, Jupiter, Saturn, Mercury and Venus are mostly direct in motion but turn retrograde periodically**.

It can also be seen that the tara grahas turn retrograde when they are at their closest to planet Earth as this is the time when they lap or get lapped by Earth during their journey around the Sun.

In Vedic astrology, retrograde planets are termed as *vakri grahas* (meaning twisted or crooked).

We will primarily be studying the impact of the retrograde motion of Mercury, Venus, Mars, Jupiter and Saturn in this book.

Impact of Retrograde Planets on a Horoscope

Planets in retrograde motion are given high levels of importance in Vedic astrology. This is because of their movement across the zodiac signs in an anticlockwise direction which is against convention.

The primary term once can use for retrograde planets is

The concept of retrograde planets holds very high levels of significance in Vedic astrology. After all, planets like human beings *(natives)* are entities which are constantly on the move. In addition to the intrinsic traits that they exhibit, their behavior undergoes change as they travel in a particular direction across the zodiacs and when that direction is altered, so is their behavior which ultimately leads to unexpected outcomes.

This is what happens when a planet which is supposed to be direct in motion turns retrograde. It goes against the norms or convention and becomes abnormal in its behavior. Not necessarily good or bad but uncommon.

For example, Mercury (direct in motion) placed in Mithuna rashi in the 10th house from the lagna could make the native an excellent communicator or orator which he/she could use effectively in his/her professional life to lead from the front. However, if this Mercury is retrograde, the native may be an introvert and might use this placement to become a strategist for leading think tanks or political organizations.

Following are some of the attributes of planets in retrograde motion:

1. All planets during retrogression are at their closest position from planet Earth which indicates that the planets will have greater influence on the natives.

2. Planets in retrograde motion travel faster when compared to planets in direct motion.

3. Retrograde planets have additional strength on account of their speed as a result of which their ability to do good or bad gets enhanced.

4. Natives with retrograde planets in their birth chart will be more introspective in nature which may make them turn inward and sometimes dormant or missing in action. They may seem shy, disorderly or lost at times but in many cases this may lead them to discovering something novel. Such people turn out to be great innovators.

5. The more the number of retrograde planets in your birth chart, higher is the likelihood of you facing more obstacles in your life. Remember retrograde means abnormal, so

something in your life will be out of the orderly which will cause you to undergo pain before you see the gain.

6. Retrograde motion of tara grahas is akin to these grahas being on vacation which may result in delays in the occurrence of a positive or negative event associated with these planets.

7. Retrogression is like the recoil of the gun. The individual will channelize his thoughts carefully and dig deep into his reserves before proceeding on the next step of his journey. It is like hitting a pause button.

8. **Classical texts in Vedic astrology have reiterated the fact that planets that are retrograde (with the exception of Rahu and Ketu) indicate some unfinished business from your past life. There is karma carried over from your previous birth which you will have to fulfill in this lifetime.** We will discuss this more when we study the retrograde motion of the tara grahas.

Chart 1 (Rashi Chart):

<table>
<tr><td rowspan="1">Meena</td><td colspan="2">——Direct——→
Mesha | Vrishaba
←Retrograde—</td><td>Mithuna</td></tr>
<tr><td>Kumbha</td><td colspan="2" rowspan="2"></td><td>Kataka</td></tr>
<tr><td>Makara</td><td>Simha</td></tr>
<tr><td>Dhanu</td><td>Vrischika</td><td>Tula</td><td>Kanya</td></tr>
</table>

Mesha rashi to Vrishaba rashi = Direct Motion
Vrishaba rashi to Mesha rashi = Retrograde Motion

Table No. 1: Frequency of Retrogression and its Impact:

Planet	Frequency of Occurrence	Number of Days in Retrograde Motion in a year	Longitudinal Distance from Sun	Element	Impact
Mercury	Thrice a year (Every 116 days)	~21-25 days	14-20°	Earth	Natural calamities, poverty, accidents
Venus	2 times in 3 years (Every 584 days)	~43 days	28°	Water	Change in thinking, Emotional imbalance
Mars	Once in 2 years (Every 780 days)	~60-80 days	220-230°	Fire	Wars, Separation in family life
Jupiter	Once a year (Every 399 days)	~120 days	245°	Sky/ Ether	Misfortune
Saturn	Once a year (Every 378 days)	~140 days	251°	Air	Trouble in relationships

Chapter 2

Retrograde Movement of Tara Grahas

Retrograde Mercury:

We have seen in chapter 1 that Mercury is one of the planets of the solar system that retrogrades periodically when it orbits the Sun.

Refer 'Table No. 1' where we mention the frequency of occurrence and the number of days it spends in retrograde motion. This translates into approximately 20% of the year when Mercury is vakri meaning 20% of the world's population would have a retrograde Mercury in their horoscope.

Mercury meaning mercurial or changeable is the fastest moving planet in the solar system taking just 88 days to complete revolution around the Sun. In Vedic astrology, it signifies communication, speech, intelligence, business, trading, mathematics, technology and writing. (Refer the book titled, "Vedic Astrology: A Journey Through History, Principles and Mathematical Foundations" for more details).

Retrograde Mercury makes the native an introvert and inward looking. Such individuals will find it difficult to communicate their feelings for fear of being misunderstood. They may not be the sociable types and would prefer to live their lives in their own space. On the other hand, retrograde Mercury allows these individuals to deal with abstract concepts, observe and discover patterns, and solve complex problems which people with a direct Mercury in their birth chart cannot. Mercury rules over the mind and retrograde Mercury will these individuals possess a powerful sub-conscious mind. They may know a lot more than what they can communicate which sometimes can lead them to feeling very frustrated.

On the flip side, retrograde Mercury makes the native with a powerful sub-conscious mind a creative genius. Verbal communication may be a problem but many individuals with retrograde Mercury excel in professions that require non-verbal communication. Musicians, dancers, painters, directors, designers, tech entrepreneurs, innovators and scientists are examples of professionals who are likely to have retrograde Mercury in their horoscope.

Finally, as I mentioned earlier, a planet being retrograde indicates impact of your actions or karma from your previous birth which you will have to fulfill in this lifetime. For example, Retrograde Mercury could imply that in your past life, you may have been a powerful orator who through his public speeches incensed a riot ultimately leading to a war like situation. It could be that you escaped unnoticed for your role. In this birth, you may find a number of obstacles coming in your way when you air your views in a public platform or even at a small social gathering. The Mercury here is going to make you think long and hard before you decide talk in public.

Needless to say, Retrograde Mercury will confer varying results when placed in different zodiac signs and different houses (bhavas). Let us briefly look at possible outcomes.

Table No. 2: Impact of Retrograde Mercury on various Rashis and Bhavas:

	Rashi	Results	House (Bhava)	Results
Impact of placement of Retrograde Mercury in	Mesha	Rash, impatient, Intuitive leader of men.	1st	Tends to talk quickly and gets into trouble.
	Vrishaba	Practical but selfish, Desires praise.	2nd	Native may tend to stammer while speaking (This is the house of speech). Selfish but lavish.
	Mithuna	introvert. Communicates unconventionally.	3rd	Indicates a research scientist. Patient thinker.
	Kataka	Emotional, Introspective, Diffident, Philosopher, Trader of luxury goods.	4th	Obstacles in obtaining properties, conveyances, education. Could get sudden inheritance.
	Simha	Artist, Invents new games and sports, Action oriented, Invests a lot of time in his hobbies.	5th	Intellectual. Wants to be a leader. Hasty risk taker, gambler, trader, Good with games that require concentration.
	Kanya	Exalted Mercury. Native will be a talented research scientist, sportsman, artist, inventor, discoverer.	6th	Quarrels and conflicts at workplace due to unconventional approach. Perfectionist.

	Tula	Associated with media, entertainment, dance, theatre. Could be a director.	7th	Unconventional marriage (Native rushes into marriage without giving it a thought or may deliberate too much before taking the plunge).
	Vrischika	Skilled surgeon, military personnel.	8th	May cause unnatural death but can give long life, wealth, wisdom. Again a researcher.
	Dhanu	Religious preacher, Innovative educationist, Discoverer of lands and faiths.	9th	Unconventional education, Thought leader, preacher, Hasty in action at times.
	Makara	Politician, Skilled scientist, Out of the box thinker, Inventor.	10th	Sudden gains in profession (Business and Politics).
	Kumbha	Founder and head of novel organization.	11th	Unexpected gains from friends an elder siblings.
	Meena	Debilitated. Dreamy, Bouts of depression and lack of self-belief.	12th	Investigative officer, Psychological in nature, Trouble with sleep patterns.

Example 1:

	Rahu	Asc Jupiter	
			Moon
			Venus
Saturn		Mars Ketu	Sun Mercury (R)

Above is the birth chart of a popular and famous playback singer in the entertainment industry. The native has Vrishaba lagna rising at the time of birth. Mercury is retrograde **(Note the 'R' in the birth chart. Rahu and Ketu are always retrograde as a result of which we don't suffix the 'R' in their case)** or vakri and is placed in the 5th house in conjunction with Sun in Kanya rashi. Mercury is exalted in this sign. The native was born in Ashalesha nakshatra in Kataka rashi (Moon in Kataka rashi).

Retrograde Mercury made the native an introvert but she used this placement effectively to build a career in the entertainment industry as a playback singer. Remember, Mercury is vakri in the 5th house in Kanya rashi which means the native may excel in a form of communication that is creative and not conventional but which at the same time requires very high levels of concentration.

Also, in this chart the 10th house owner, Saturn, is aspecting the 5th house indicating the native will take up a hobby and make it her profession. All major events in the native's life happened during either the dasha or antardasha (bhukti) of Mercury.

She entered the field of cinema and singing early at the age of 13 when she was passing through the period of

Mercury dasha Jupiter bhukti. Through sheer perseverance, determination and god given talent, she overcome all the obstacles in the competitive world of entertainment and rose to the zenith of her profession. The 10th lord, Saturn is yogakaarak and its placement in 8th house and aspect on 5th house indicates a lengthy career and a long lifespan. The conjunction of Sun with Mercury made her achieve worldwide fame. During the period of Venus dasha Mercury bhukti she was honored by the government of India with Padma-Bhushan and during Rahu dasha Mercury bhukti she received the highest civilian award of Bharat-Ratna. Mercury was clearly the major driver in shaping the life of this individual.

Example 2:

	Ketu Sun	Mercury (R) Saturn	Venus
			Jupiter Mars
		Rahu Moon	Asc

This chart is that of a former president of a leading superpower. Again Mercury is retrograde in the 9th house in Vrishaba rashi and is conjunct with Saturn which owns the 6th house of conflicts and enemies. Mercury owns the 1st house and 10th house of profession is clearly the most important planet is this horoscope. Not surprisingly the native became president of his country during the period of Mercury dasha Saturn bhukti. But the retrograde Mercury placed in the 9th house and afflicted by Saturn made the native take the most inhuman decision of dropping atom bombs on Hiroshima and Nagasaki in Japan. A combination of Mercury in Vrishaba rashi and 9th house influence made him take this decision in haste without considering the fallout of such an action. Later on, the native in the mahadasha of Ketu ushered in many economic reforms and helped in the formation of the United Nations.

Retrograde Venus:

The planet of Venus retrogrades roughly 41 to 45 days in a year which means about 12% of the world's population will have a retrograde Venus in their birth chart.

Venus is the planet of beauty, love, comforts and luxuries, entertainment, wealth, sexuality, fine arts, cinema and theatre. It is of course the planet of romantic relationships and chief significator for marriages. When Venus turns retrograde, all of the above attributes and significations are called into question. A retrograde Venus indicates complexities or stress involved in romantic relationships with your love interests or with your spouse. It could mean you may be finding it difficult to express your love and affection towards your significant other. Perhaps your soul is carrying the memories of painful relationships that you have endured in your past life. Likewise, Venus which also is one of main significator planets for financial stability, if retrograde, could lead the native to take complex and impetuous decisions with regards to money matters.

The above may happen in several ways. It might be that in your past life, you had a misunderstanding with your spouse and for no fault of his/hers, you decided to leave him/her for another. This means that in your current birth, bad karma will pay you back. You might be accused of sexual misconduct which may land you in trouble with the authorities despite being innocent. Or you may end up marrying someone from a different faith or belief and live to regret it for the rest of your life. In both ways, retrograde Venus has given you a punishment even though your actions seemed straightforward in this lifetime.

The same can happen with matters of finance. You have deceived a moneylender by not paying him back his dues in your previous birth. Karma might even out by a bank filing false money laundering case against you.

Of course, retrograde Venus alone doesn't guarantee the occurrence of any negative event. Other factors such as its placement in a particular rashi or bhava need to be gauged. In retrogression, Venus can reward you also by giving handsome financial returns on an investment that you never thought would make money for you.

Natives with retrograde Venus, like in case of Mercury, will be introverts and will carefully think through the merits and de-merits before entering into a romantic relationship or taking decisions for their financial well-being. They prefer quality control and life full of happiness when compared to materialism. On the other hand, due to the higher velocity of motion during retrogression, some may even rush into decisions which may cause them high levels of stress later.

Retrograde, as we saw at the beginning of this book, means unconventional or abnormal. Thus people with retrograde Venus may use an out of the box approach in solving problems in their personal and professional life. For example, an actor who had made a name for himself in the cinema world by playing the lead role in action flicks and who is experiencing a lull in his career graph may successfully switch to playing lead roles in romantic comedies, resulting in him attaining stratospheric levels of success.

Table No. 3: Impact of Retrograde Venus on various Rashis and Bhavas:

	Rashi	Results	House (Bhava)	Results
Impact of placement of Retrograde Venus in	Mesha	In the sign of it enemy Mars. Native might be shy in expressing his emotions. There is fear of rejection.	1st	Will have desire to be like Jonathan Livingston seagull. Media baron.
	Vrishaba	Sensuous by nature. Could be a spendthrift.	2nd	Focused on family affairs. Can be dominating. Obstacles in wealth creation but can be very rich.
	Mithuna	May not appear sociable and communicative. May appear cool on the exterior but could in fact be very warm and caring.	3rd	Upachaya house. Improves with age. Literary artist.
	Kataka	Water sign so very emotional and sensitive. People may not know how caring they are until they get to know them. Moon's rashi so good placement to become singer-songwriter, music composer.	4th	Venus is digbali here. So it's comfortable but retrograde meaning it will want to standout in the crowd. Choice of life partner after much deliberation. Very careful in investments.

	Simha	May become loyal to the wrong set of individuals. Timid in matters of love, beauty, and money. Can be gregarious but it's not visible.	5th	Love marriage. Spouse could belong to a different religion or culture. Very careful in approach. Can make a good CEO.
	Kanya	Debilitated. Can develop unusual attraction and fixation. May find it hard in letting go. Difficulty in moving on from break-ups.	6th	Confrontation in relationships. Stormy equation with lenders/financiers. Rebellious.
	Tula	Indecisive in relationships. Need for closeness and companionship in love.	7th	Either too many companions or none. Trouble in life on account of partners. Can get sudden riches in business.
	Vrischika	Intense need for privacy. Will try and stick around in partnerships even if things are going downhill.	8th	If not afflicted can give a lengthy life. Trouble over inheritance and property disputes. Hallucinations. A dreamer.
	Dhanu	Popular but dissatisfied internally.	9th	Spouse can be from a foreign culture. Lots of obstacles before choosing a partner. Can be attracted to another faith.

	Makara	Friendly sign. Expectations rise with success and can get to head. Not good for partnerships if native is a perfectionist.	10th	Artistic innovator. Liberalist. Deals in luxury goods. Can have multiple sources of income.
	Kumbha	Big network of acquaintances. Might go for unconventional relationships.	11th	Unconventional married life (eg: Big age difference with spouse) May have many partners or may prefer a live-in. Gains from foreign lands.
	Meena	Exalted. Dreamy and romanticizes the past. Awkward externally but compassionate inward.	12th	Idealistic. Loss in relationships. Inter-caste marriage. Disconnect in romantic life on account of faulty selection of partner.

Example 3:

	Mars		Ketu Saturn (R)
Asc			Moon
Venus (R) Jupiter			
Rahu Sun Mercury			

Above is the birth chart of a leading cine star. Native is popular and has had a very successful period in the entertainment industry. He has Kumbha lagna with lagna lord,

Saturn, placed in the 5th house. Note Saturn is retrograde. He had a difficult childhood and was made fun of at school. Native is Ashalesha nakshatra, Kataka rashi with Moon being placed in the 6th house. This indicates, the native will always have worries throughout even if it turns out to be something very trivial.

Venus, the karaka for entertainment and romantic relationships, is placed in the 12th house of losses but for Kumbha lagna natives, it is also the yogakaarak planet, meaning it can give stratospheric success. Clearly, Venus is highly significant planet is this horoscope.

The native has the 5th lord Mercury and 7th lord Sun conjunct in the 11th house, indicating love marriage. Not surprisingly, the native married his childhood sweetheart in an inter-religious wedding ceremony during the period of Venus dasha Rahu bhukti. He also made his debut in the world of cinema as a lead star in the same Venus-Rahu period. Thus, retrograde Venus gave him both a livelihood and personal joy. Unfortunately, as Venus was placed in the 12th house of losses with Sun and Mercury afflicted by Saturn, he separated from his wife and got divorced during the period of Venus dasha Mercury bhukti.

Thus, Venus gave him name and fame, but its unfavorable placement meant that he couldn't understand the true meaning of love which resulted in his marriage getting terminated.

Example 4:

		Ketu	
			Mars Jupiter Mercury
			Saturn Sun
	Asc Rahu	Moon	Venus (R)

Native was a highly acclaimed author of her time. Lagna lord Mars is debilitated in the 9th house indicating a number of unpleasant incidents in personal life. Moon in Swati nakshatra in Tula rashi is placed in the 12th house also indicating a troubled mind. Venus is retrograde in the 11th house but is debilitated.

She lost her mother at the age of 11 when she was passing through the period of Jupiter dasha Venus bhukti. In the same period her marriage was arranged though it did not take place till she was 16. At the age of 41 when she was running the period of Mercury dasha Venus bhukti she left her husband and chose to enter into a live-in relationship with a man 10 years younger to her. Venus being debilitated and retrograde meant she had problems in marriage and chose an unconventional approach which shocked her community. Venus in 11th house indicates multiple relationships. Placement of 12th owner in 11th house indicates a loss followed by a gain.

Retrograde Mars:

Mars is the planet of action, courage, war, self-confidence, leadership abilities. It is a warrior planet which is known to give, energy, drive, determination, physical strength and risk taking abilities. Professions connected to Mars will always have the element of risk, security, danger and physical effort involved. Sportspersons, politicians and government officials, military personnel, doctors and surgeons will all have an influential Mars in their birth chart.

When Mars turns retrograde, the native may be timid, lacking in self-direction and may have other self-imposed emotional obstacles which will hold them back from realizing his/her dreams. The path to glory will be full of obstacles especially for those connected to Mars related professions. Such people will find it difficult to express themselves in a clear and firm manner. Anger can build up over a period of time causing them to implode and as a result be very harsh on others. This could result in over-aggressive behavior at the workplace which will cause further conflicts and give them a bad reputation. Native may lack sex-drive or may have very high levels of libido.

Mars retrograde however, is also an opportunity to channelize your frustrations for the greater good. Remember, retrograde means the ability to spot patterns that others can't. People with retrograde Mars could turn out to be excellent crisis managers especially during times of wars, conflicts and corporate battles. Their personality and their own struggles can be used to douse the fire before it gets out of control. They will be make good spies and can solve problems related to bio-terrorism. They may come out with vaccinations to solve global pandemic problems.

Mars is retrograde in your horoscope because of unfinished karma from your past life. It is quite possible that in your previous birth you were a soldier in the military who performed regrettable acts on the orders of someone. This may have filled you with guilt. In your current lifetime, you will have to cleanse this bad karma and life may take you down a path where you play the role of a negotiator in resolving a long standing border dispute that has torn apart two nation states or even communities. Accusations may be hurled at you for not being a fair arbiter although you have maintained neutrality throughout. Retrograde Mars could also mean that in your previous birth, you were involved in grabbing land parcels from innocent civilians without proper authorization. In this lifetime, you might be needlessly dragged into land disputes.

Unfinished karma can also be in the form of a sports person who in his previous birth had his career cut short unfairly through evil machinations of the system, thus not getting his due. In this lifetime, he may become an iconic athlete who the world reveres. He may have originally been a sprint racer but after a career threatening injury, instead of hanging up his boots, he may switched his attention to running marathons thereby earning worldwide fame and adulation. So karma, can pay you back in a good way also.

The planet of Mars retrogrades roughly 60-80 days once every 2 years which means about 10% of the world's population will have a retrograde Mars in their birth chart.

Table No. 4: Impact of Retrograde Mars on various Rashis and Bhavas:

	Rashi	Results	House (Bhava)	Results
Impact of placement of Retrograde Mars in	Mesha	Introvert, unsocial but can use retrogression to regroup energy to solve problems. Great placement for sports persons, military commanders.	1st	Native always fights for a cause. Can be extra-libidinous, aggressive, boastful and quarrelsome by nature. If aggression controlled, then native can be a popular rebel who fights for people's freedom. Justice seeker.
	Vrishaba	Disinterested. Lacks intuition. Causes turbulence in domestic matters and health.	2nd	Too materialistic. Doesn't value beauty. Might have accumulated wealth through unscrupulous means in previous birth. This may create impediments in current lifetime.

	Mithuna	Problems in romantic relationships. Issues with communication and working in a group. If overcome can be a great investigator or a businessman. Many hobbies, desires and dreams but lacks focus.	3rd	Issues with siblings. Wavering mind. Lacks self-discipline and can be rash. Mood swings can result in native being aloof from near and dear ones. Can use these defects, however, to become a powerful orator.
	Kataka	Debilitated. Emotional turmoil. Issues on the professional front especially for those in public life. Problem with property business. Can lose energy very quickly. Issues with family life.	4th	Like a ring-master. Strict disciplinarian. Wants to make sure emotions don't get the better of him. Unable to open up. Can be a great mentor, life coach and psychologist to future generations.
	Simha	Good placement to be a leader among men but can be dictatorial because of obstacles faced early on in life. Can lack self-confidence.	5th	House of romance, children and entertainment. Unconventional sex life. Baggage with respect to opposite sex from previous Impediments may make him leave projects unfinished. Will love to travel and always be on the go birth. Can be aggressive towards friends.

	Kanya	Can affect the finances of the native and decisions related to trading and investments. Partnership business may go bust. Good for abstract topics. Native makes a good psychoanalyst.	6th	Prone to disease and accidents because of impetuous nature of Mars. Can defeat his enemies easily.
	Tula	Must pay attention to suppressed and forgotten desires. Lack of enthusiasm in partnerships and romantic relationships leading to miscommunication. Native must know what he wants from companions.	7th	Had used marriage and business and gains in previous life. Could have abnormal marital life. Maybe multiple marriages.
	Vrischika	Good placement for excellence in sports. Native however may have many secret worries and suffers from health setbacks. As a result, energy remains low and native suffers from self-belief.	8th	Past life might have ended through violence, quarrels, and disputes. Might have scammed someone for money. Native doesn't trust anyone. Can grow in life through tact and diplomacy. Spirituality will help. Large inheritance and riches through in-laws indicated.

	Dhanu	Affects creative abilities, hobbies, entertainment and children. Can be a great mystery novelist or financial whiz kid.	9th	Might not respect religious beliefs or might be a dangerous fanatic. Needs to be spiritual. Long distance journeys and spiritual retreats may help.
	Makara	Exalted. Can be very dominating which affects family life and rapport with colleagues. Needs to control his anger. Great for sportsman, surgeons, and army chiefs.	10th	Wants professional success at any cost. Conduct in previous lifetime might have been good but been self-centered. In current birth, people may not respect him although they will acknowledge his success. Can be a good surgeon, physician, military general or high ranking government official.
	Kumbha	Can be over-enthusiastic without being able to express himself. Affects relationship with siblings, neighbors and circle of friends. Some people use it to their advantage to take precautions and move forward in a practical way. Loner and nature lover.	11th	Gives importance to friends but may want to push through his agenda, disregarding their viewpoint.

	Meena	Child-like and jovial but in a rash manner. Affects matters of life such as personal finances, land, property, conveyances. Needs to be very prudent. Can achieve a lot of success.	12th	Keeps poor health. Has psychological problems and doubts in expressing himself. If native has ability to moderate his personal woes, can use this to become a counselor or healer.

Example 5:

	Mars (R) Saturn (R)	Jupiter (R)	
Moon Ketu			Asc
Sun Mercury Venus (R)			Rahu

Native is a world famous sportsman revered by all. Lagna lord Moon is placed in 8th house indicating mind is full of worries. Four of the five tara grahas are retrograde, indicating life will be full of

obstacles. There is a heavy dosage of past life karma embedded in this horoscope. 10th owner Mars is placed in its own house in vakri, forming a powerful Ruchaka yoga. Thus, Mars turned out to be the primary driver for success in this birth chart. The native had to put up with various forms of racial abuse as he hailed from the African American community. However, he didn't allow this to deter and instead used it to his advantage to defend himself by taking up boxing. During the period of Rahu dasha Mars bhukti he won gold medal at the

Olympics. He was suspended from the boxing ring and jailed for not joining the armed forces during the Vietnam War but bounced back by winning the world heavyweight boxing title during the period of Jupiter dasha Mars bhukti. 7th house was afflicted by influence of 3 retrograde planets (Jupiter, Venus and Saturn) and thus he married multiple times. Affliction on 9th lord Venus meant he changed his religion. During the period of Saturn dasha Mars bhukti he was diagnosed with Parkinson's disease which ultimately claimed his life.

Retrograde Jupiter:

Jupiter is the largest planet of our solar system. He is the advisor or teacher to the Devas. Given its weight Jupiter has a tendency to expand everything in our life including body weight, speech, financial worth, family and progeny. It is the planet of optimism, knowledge, education, good fortune, long distance journeys, wealth, wisdom and general growth in all walks of life. It can bestow name, fame and honor if favorably placed. Vocations connected to Jupiter include higher education, professors, banking and financial services, legal matters and law, philosophy, faith, religion and religious preaching, philosophy, government advisory and ministers.

When Jupiter turns retrograde, all the above significations get affected. It can be seen from the above that Jupiter is the planet of expansion. Thus when Jupiter is retrograde in your birth chart, you will feel a sense of restriction in your life with respect to your body, mind and soul. Plans go haywire. Projects get delayed. Your guides or teachers turn hostile towards you. Banks may suddenly stop lending to you or procrastinate because of issues at their end. A court that was supposed to rule in your favor might postpone the judgment because the judge has suddenly taken ill.

Retrograde Jupiter could also make the native question cherished religious beliefs although he himself may not be a disbeliever and may just feel a lack of spiritual contentment. There is continuous analysis and reevaluation of the old moral, religious, spiritual values of the society. He may understand the value of education but may not involve himself in long term deep studies. The native's energy turns inward in a bid develop himself internally to seek the truth. He will be independent and not want to follow in the footsteps of others.

As in the case of other planets, retrograde Jupiter in one's birth chart indicates good or bad effects of past life karma. The native will have to face a number of obstacles. In the previous birth, the native may have been an economist who stole another professor's idea and unfairly used it to gain worldwide acclaim. This might come back to bite him in his current life where he gets criticized and targeted for developing a novel technology product which can benefit millions but which his colleagues see as a waste of time. He will have to work harder to prove that his idea is worth its weight in gold. Will be a game changer.

People with retrograde Jupiter turn out to be great thinkers and philosophers who come out with revolutionary ideas that can enhance the quality of human life either spiritually or materialistically.

Ultimately their soul and mind takes them along a path where they turn out to be game changers. They are born leaders. This placement is good for scientists, tech innovators, captains in team sports, prime ministers/presidents of nation states, authors, spiritual gurus and god men, artists, industrialists.

Jupiter retrogrades once a year for a period of 120 days. Thus, about 32% of the world's population will have retrograde Jupiter in its birth chart.

Table No. 5: Impact of Retrograde Jupiter on various Rashis and Bhavas:

	Rashi	Results	House (Bhava)	Results
Impact of placement of Retrograde Jupiter in	Mesha	The native may not be friendly and lacks nobility and empathy. Can affect relationship with family members and society. Disciplines lifestyle will help alleviate problems.	1st	Can go on long distance journeys and pilgrimages. Could result in wasteful expenditure.
	Vrishaba	Affects timely decision making ability. Lacks tact. Self-centered but can use this placement to focus on an important task to complete it on time.	2nd	Native will want to keep financial matters under strict control. Health setbacks possible. Disturbances in family life should be dealt with patience.
	Mithuna	Ambivalent mind. Judgment on matters pertaining to finances and property investment called into question. Needs to assess the situation carefully. Slowing down the process may help. Good position for innovators.	3rd	Retrograde Jupiter can give very good results. Sudden gains possible. Good for speculation and short distance journeys. Can help with communicating new ideas.

	Kataka	Exalted. May become too sentimental or lacks emotion completely. Might result in flawed decision making at the highest level. Good for professions connected to agriculture and fine arts. Good for industrialists.	4th	Native has to put extra-effort to achieve his goals. Can give sudden elevation in career. Might have many properties and conveyances. Suffers from lifestyle diseases like obesity.
	Simha	Native may take a wrong decision in haste and live to regret it later. Lack of sleep and bed-pleasures. Needs to turn to spirituality.	5th	Gives good results in all walks of life except with respect to children. Good for entertainment industry.
	Kanya	Gives mixed results here. Can affect health and give many adversaries. If used wisely, very good placement for traders and businessman.	6th	Can create lots of adversaries and unwanted expenditures in foreign lands if reckless. Good for government jobs.
	Tula	Can give material growth and happiness but flawed decision making skills can result in run-ins with superior officers.	7th	Good for marriage and business partnerships but remember, decisions must be made after careful deliberation.

	Vrischika	Can turn out to be selfish. Needs to approach every problem with a mindset of for the greater good of humanity. Good placement for captains of team based sports. Avoid blind faith in religious matters.	8th	Occurrence of events are sudden. Must avoid rash behavior. Sudden inflow of wealth indicated. Accident prone. If not afflicted, can give long life.
	Dhanu	Jupiter's own house. Gives good results. Truth seeker. Connects with noble and high dignitaries. Inclined to religious and good deeds. Can make for a great judge or bureaucrat or politician.	9th	Good for long distance journeys, spiritual seekers and pilgrimages, occult activities. Needs to put in lot of effort to succeed.
	Makara	Debilitated. Can surprisingly be a good period for marriage and business partnerships. Again native should not be self-centered. Should be careful in professional field.	10th	Can give good results in professional sphere after a lot of hard work. Good for sportsmen, politicians, and cinema stars alike.

	Kumbha	Apart from odd health setbacks and tough environment at the workplace, this placement can give native lots of success if practices detachment and spirituality.	11th	All-round gains if native is willing to take additional responsibilities and leadership role even if he is not fully ready. Focus should be on the masses and the good of humanity.
	Meena	Own house. Can develop good sentiments and feelings. Gives good academic results and family life. Native has strong intuitive ability. Good placement for traders, businessman and explorers.	12th	Unnecessary household expenditures, delays and setbacks in professional projects. Exposure to occult sciences. Worries with regard to children.

Example 6:

Moon	Mars		Ketu Jupiter(R)
Sun			
Mercury(R)			Asc
Rahu Venus		Saturn	

Native was a computer visionary and one of the greatest inventors of the 20th and 21st century. He is known as the father of the personal computer revolution in the 1970s and 80s. The native was Simha lagna which made him a born leader of men. Moon's placement in the 8th house in Meena rashi (Uttarabhadrapada nakshatra) and retrograde Mercury meant the native had several health setbacks in life and didn't possess the strongest body constitution. Jupiter retrograde in 11th house along with Mercury retrograde in 6th house meant the native was a creative out-of-the-box thinker who wanted to use science and technology for the betterment of human life. Remember Jupiter retrograde in 11th house means the native thinks about the good of humanity. Jupiter in Mithuna rashi meant he was good at communicating his ideas. Jupiter's aspect on Venus and Rahu placed in the 5th house meant the native had a flair for electronics and computers from a young age. He loved building tools and developing tech products. During the period of Mercury dasha Jupiter bhukti, he and his friend developed a blue box which allowed free long-distance calls to be made. In the subsequent Ketu mahadasha, native and his friend founded a software company which today is a global tech giant. The native was at the forefront of PC revolution during the late 70s and early 80s and during the period of Ketu dasha Jupiter bhukti his firm hit a market value of $100 million. Despite this success, differences with other executives resulted in him being forced to resign from the company during the period of Venus dasha Sun bhukti. However, during the period of Venus dasha Jupiter bhukti he bounced by back by taking over the reins of the company he founded and turned it around into the tech giant it is today by developing a series of revolutionary products including the most celebrated smartphone. Unfortunately, his ill-health came back to dog him and he ultimately died of pancreatic cancer during the period of Moon dasha Jupiter bhukti.

Example 7:

		Jupiter(R)	Ketu
			Asc
Moon			Mars
Rahu Venus	Sun Mercury (R)	Saturn	

Native was a powerful prime minister of her country and was popular among the masses. Lagna lord Moon is placed in the 7th house. The birth chart has 2 planets Mercury and Jupiter in retrograde and aspecting each other, indicating breaks in formal education or the lack of it. The native didn't face the mahadasha of Mercury but the mahadasha of Jupiter turned out to be a life changing experience for her. Jupiter owns the 6th house of adversaries and the 9th house of father and good fortune. She was elected president of her party during the period of Jupiter dasha, Saturn bhukti. She lost her father during the period of Jupiter dasha Venus bhukti (9th lord retrograde indicates loss of father in its period) but good fortune smiled on her when despite not being the leading candidate of her party she managed to get a majority of the party's elected representatives to rally behind her and became prime minister of her country during the period of Jupiter dasha Sun bhukti. Sun, the significator for prestige, fame and position in politics was being aspected by retrograde Jupiter indicating a sudden and rather surprising elevation to the top job. Jupiter's ownership of 6th house meant lot of obstacles and enmity in her chosen line of profession but its ownership of the 9th house meant that good fortune smiled on her as she reached the pinnacle of her profession. In the subsequent period of Jupiter dasha Moon bhukti she managed to lead her party to victory in the country's general elections. Jupiter in 11th house gave her big gains during its mahadasha.

Retrograde Saturn:

Saturn is the farthest planet away from the Vedic astrology from the Sun. It is a slow moving, cold, dry and dreary planet. In astrology, it indicates, delays, sorrows, rejections, defeats, restrictions, practicality, orderliness and discipline, the elderly, defensiveness, secretive behavior. Now, some of the above words are feared by human beings in general as anything that places curbs on the freedom of movements and happiness is met with contempt and rebellion at times by human beings. But Saturn in reality is trying to bring a structure in your life through a methodical approach that can help you climb ladders in life, one step at a time. It is the planet of practicality and realism which is actually trying instill in you qualities of patience, persistence, determination and organizational capabilities which is why those with a very strong Saturn climb turn out to be leaders who can influence an entire nation or the human race as such.

Natives with retrograde Saturn may delve into the realms of their sub-conscious mind to get to resolve issues. This unfortunately at times can lead them to developing a defeatist attitude. They let external pressures get the better of them and are not able to make best use of their capabilities to progress in life. They are shy, introverts and lack self-confidence. Again communication turns out to be an issue both in personal and professional relationships. They feel that the universe is deliberately avoiding them and conspiring against them. On the other hand, if they channelize thee energy of the retrograde planet, they turn out to be among the most sought after individuals both on the intellectual as well as the spiritual side. They can make great presidents of their nation or CEO of a large multinational corporation particularly in the heavy industry and petroleum sectors because they demonstrate qualities such as patience, meticulous planning, perseverance and organizational abilities. Such people however can regularly have conflicts with higher authorities, and heads of organizations and nations for their contrarian views.

Saturn is the planet of karma. Needless to say, retrograde Saturn indicates karma carried over from your past life time. This could be either positive of negative. It is possible that you were a monarch in your previous lifetime who ill-treated his subjects while lording over riches and worldly comforts while the people burnt in despair. In this lifetime, the native may be a born into a family of modest means and despite possessing worldly talents will find impediments at each step of his professional life with a number of adversaries who will be keen to prevent his rise. This is more likely in professions connected to the masses such as politics, government and bureaucracy, media and entertainment, applied science and engineering, aviation and petroleum industries. It is also possible that the native was a renowned scientist in his previous birth who passed away tragically in an accident. In this lifetime, he may be born a child prodigy who gains a postdoc by the time he turns 13 and comes with a novel approach to reduce emission of greenhouse gases in the atmosphere.

Saturn stays in retrograde motion for 140 days every year which means that approximately 36% of the world's population has retrograde Saturn in its horoscope.

Table No. 6: Impact of Retrograde Saturn on various Rashis and Bhavas:

	Rashi	Results	House (Bhava)	Results
Impact of placement of Retrograde Saturn in	Mesha	Debilitated. Comes across as rude and impolite. Can be a strict disciplinarian but also quite arrogant. Can be a great scientist or rational thinker.	1st	Difficulty in airing his views early on in life. Native has strong will-power and can rise to the top despite setbacks. Good for public life.
	Vrishaba	Can face obstacles in wealth accumulation but through hard-work can rise to the top. Materialistic in nature.	2nd	Emotional disconnect. Financial difficulties. Steady accumulation of wealth. Family life better in the 2nd half of life after initial days of lack of creature comforts. Goody for movie directors.
	Mithuna	Imaginative but can be a hypocrite. Might try and game the system.	3rd	Responsibility could come at an early age. Introvert but opens up gradually. Good for speculators. Gains through short journeys. Investigative ability.

	Kataka	Very sentimental yet very hard-working. Can be very popular with the masses. Life is full professional hurdles but can make it to the top. Unorthodox in nature. Good for sportsman, artists, creators and politicians.	4th	Attached to motherly figure. Obstacles in promotion in professional life on account of aspect on 10th house. Can affect health. Travels in foreign lands.
	Simha	Born leader. Unconventional entrepreneur. New-age warrior. Responsible towards father figure. Can become very rich. Delays and disappointments in matters of romance and marriage.	5th	Affects romance, education and children. Speculation in stock markets and casinos can lead to huge losses. Needs to regroup creative abilities and views regarding entertainment.
	Kanya	Health setbacks. Finds it difficult to execute tasks according to a plan. Succeeds in life through sustained hard work. Responsible towards family.	6th	Health problems. Can perform immoral acts. Aggressive. Good organizational capabilities. Ability to work hard. Can win over enemies. Very ambitious.

	Tula	Exalted. Gives opportunity to live in foreign land. Causes delays and problems in marriage. Native could be a spendthrift and has doubtful nature. Has to be careful on partnerships.	7th	Delays marriage but marriage can bring good luck to him. Could have had many affairs prior to the marriage. Finds faults with others.
	Vrischika	Native can be prone to violence and accidents. May get chronic illness. Can give huge inheritance and voracious will-power to succeed in fields connected to science and technology.	8th	Afraid of joint ventures, investments and expressions of sexual desires. Native can be very learned and changes old and traditional ways. Good for all professions if used wisely. Usually an explorer or discoverer.
	Dhanu	Can make the native cultured, peaceful, honest and honorable. Could be a spiritual thinker. Trouble in foreign lands also indicated. Ideal for god-men, speculators and traders.	9th	Obstinate. Careless. Success later on in life in spheres of religion and philosophy. Inventor, spiritual guru.

	Makara	Rises to the top in professional life through sheer perseverance and hard work. Has leadership qualities but can be arrogant which could lead to his downfall. Good for politics.	10th	House of profession. Cautious in approach. Success in second part of life. May ignore his duties and abuse power.
	Kumbha	Could give explosive results. Native may talk about spirituality and religion but is busy acquiring material gains. Good for sportsmen and revolutionaries.	11th	Shy and takes time to open up. Only then will he get many friends. This however helps him to gauge people and places before coming to a conclusion. Somewhat obstinate with family and friends. Good with analysis. Likes to be praised. Could be a lawyer or an artist.
	Meena	Too sentimental. Gives and health and financial setbacks. Honorable and tactful. Spiritual mindset will help the native.	12th	Expenditures, secret enemies. Spiritual and likes to travel on pilgrimages and faraway lands.

Example 8:

		Moon	Venus
Ketu			Mercury Sun
Asc Saturn (R) Jupiter (R)			Rahu Mars

Native came from a modest background. Both his parents were academicians but divorced early on in his life. He went onto become President of his country. Lagna lord Saturn is retrograde in the 1st house and so is Jupiter. Mutual aspect of retrograde Saturn and Sun meant he had a very ordinary childhood and father was absent from his life. Mutual aspect of Mercury and 2nd lord of speech Saturn (Retrograde) meant he turned out to be an excellent orator capable of swaying the masses. Retrograde Saturn made him dig deep into his reserves and through sheer hard work and determination he got into the best colleges and became a successful lawyer. During the period of Jupiter dasha Moon bhukti he rose to the topmost job in the world that of the office of the President of the United States and was reelected for a second term by his countrymen and women during the period of Saturn dasha Saturn bhukti. Native has used the retrograde placement of both Jupiter and Saturn to his advantage in choosing a career as a public servant. He will continue to be associated with foundations and committees going forward.

Example 9:

		Saturn (R)	
Asc Ketu			Jupiter
			Rahu
		Moon	Venus Mars Mercury (R) Sun

Native is a famous and popular actor star of Bollywood. He has Kumbha lagna with lagna lord Saturn placed in the 4th house in retrograde motion. Saturn turned out to be the game changer in his life.

Placement of 4 planets in 8th house of sudden occurrences with Mars being combust, Mercury exalted, retrograde and combust and Venus debilitated gave him many ups and downs in his life. Remember, Mercury if retrograde but exalted gives the native ability to express himself in an unconventional manner (Singers, actors, dance artists, painters and sculptors). Mercury owns the 5th house of cinema, communication and creativity. Saturn's retrogression in 4th house meant the native was attached to his mother and she had a prominent role in helping him select his profession. It also affected the native's health. The native entered Bollywood during the period of Jupiter dasha Rahu bhukti and after a few initial years of struggle, delivered his first big superhit during Saturn dasha Saturn bhukti. Thereafter, he never looked back rising to be nicknamed the emperor of his industry. He also had a brief stint in politics and won his first and only election to the Indian parliament during the period of Saturn dasha Mars bhukti but couldn't sustain a career on account of combustion of 10th lord Mars. This chart is influenced more by the glamour world. Clearly, Saturn changed his life in more ways than one.

Note: The outer planets of Mars, Jupiter and Saturn retrograde when placed between the 5th and 8th sign from the Sun. For example, if Jupiter is transiting Simha rashi then, it will turn retrograde when Sun is transiting between Dhanu rashi and Meena rashi.

Chapter 3

Combust Planets

The word combust indicates something that gets burnt, consumed or destroyed by fire. We hear from time to time about large fire accidents where large swathes of land, buildings or complexes get completely razed. Increasingly commonly nowadays, we also hear about forest fires that destroy large sections of national parks affecting the livelihood of the living beings dwelling in the wild. Fire accidents have been common throughout human history whether it be at home where appliances get burnt or at the workplace where a short circuit has caused significant damage to property. Tragically, we have also witnessed or heard about rail, road and/or air accidents where people lose their lives after a great conflagration.

The same concept is applicable in Vedic astrology where grahas get burnt when they get too close to the Sun. Let us examine how this works below.

For the living beings on Earth, Sun is the ultimate source of energy and light. Quite simply, it is the giver of life. However, it is common knowledge that the heat emanating from the Sun is so strong that it burns everything that comes in its proximity (The temperature of the Sun at its surface is a whopping 6000 degrees Celsius causing any celestial object that orbits into its vicinity to be razed instantly). As a result, life cannot be sustained on the Sun as it burns or combusts any entity including planets when it goes near the Sun

In Vedic Astrology, the concept of combustion of planets or combust planets ("Asta" or even "Moudya" in Sanskrit) is a phenomenon where a planet that passes into the close orbit of the Sun, has its rays getting subdued in front of the powerful rays of the Sun. In reality, the gravitational pull will not allow the planet to get sucked into the vortex of the Sun (Thereby extinguishing the planet) but in the proximity of the Sun, the planet's rays get minimized causing them to appear invisible to an observer on Earth.

In Jyotish Shastra, this is known as the planet turning "Asta" or dark or invisible. A classic example of this is the Moon which is not visible in the sky on New Moon day (Amavasya) and the day after the New Moon day (Shukla Pratipada). On these two days, the Moon gets as close to the Sun as it can be.

Likewise, the planets of Mercury, Venus, Mars, Jupiter and Saturn also turn combust when they get too close to the Sun.

The concept of combustion do not apply to Rahu and Ketu as they are nodal points on the Moon and not real planets. In fact when Rahu or Ketu get too close to the Sun, they eclipse it. Thus, we get our annual Solar and Lunar Eclipse when Rahu or Ketu is conjunct the Sun (Moon has to be either conjunct the Sun or at the opposite point).

Example: At the time of Solar Eclipse:-

Longitude of Sun = 34°

Longitude of Moon = 34°

Longitude of Rahu = 34°

Longitude of Ketu = 214°

Moon is thus combust on Solar eclipse day.

Table No. 7: Planetary Combustion in Vedic Astrology:

Planet	Frequency of Occurrence	Number of Days in Combustion	Maximum Longitudinal Distance from Sun
Moon	Once a month	1-2 days	12°
Mercury	7 times a year (Combust 50% of the Year)	12-15 or 25-30 or 45-50 days when Direct 12-18 days when Retrograde	14° (Direct) 12° (Retrograde)
Venus	Once or twice a year	Upto 80 days when Direct 5-10 days when Retrograde	10° (Direct) 8° (Retrograde)
Mars	Once every 2 years	90-120 days	17°
Jupiter	Once a year	~30 days	11°
Saturn	Once a year	36 days	15°

Recall that when Mars, Jupiter and Saturn retrograde, they are placed somewhere in the 5th to 8th house from where the Sun is posited. Thus, they can never be both retrograde and combust at the same time. On the other hand, Venus and in particular Mercury move in close proximity to the Sun. Thus, these two inner planets can be retrograde and combust at the same time.

What is the Impact of Combust Planets?

Planets or grahas are light emitting celestial objects that impact our lives. Whenever any planet gets too close to the Sun, its rays get minimized or lost in the blazing Sun causing it to go blind. This loss of rays causes it to lose power, making it give erratic results.

So what are the effects of a planet going combust?

To answer this question we need to look at two entities, the Sun and the planet that has become combust.

Recall from the author's book titled "Vedic Astrology: A Journey Through History, Principles and Mathematical Foundations", that the Sun, which is at the center of the solar system, is the ultimate source of energy and light for all the living beings on Earth. Quite simply, it is the giver of life. It thus signifies the soul, will power and intellect, brilliance, prosperity, fame, position, success in worldly affairs, power and prestige and also our ego.

When a planet turns combust, its significations are affected adversely by the Sun's qualities causing it to give unpredictable and adverse results. This will work differently for different planets. For example, for the planet of Mercury which signifies communication, memory power and intelligence, its turning combust may make the individual have frequent memory loss. Remember, the Sun signifies the soul and thus it will impact the quality that the combust planet represents that will ultimately affect the individual on the mental plane which ultimately leads him to take random decisions. Combust planet, as a result, loses a portion of its ability to do good and doesn't give its result in entirety. Note, this is different from a planet turning retrograde which is more do with the planet's own motion. In the case of retrograde, outcome is unconventional while in the case of combust planets the results are erratic.

Table No. 8: Impact of Planetary Combustion:

Planet	Signification	Impact of Combustion
Moon	Emotions, The mind and the heart, Luxuries, Attraction, Royalty	Mental stress, Emotional breakdown, Wants luxury in all walks of life, Seeks pleasure and royalty.

Mercury	Memory power, Communication, Information processing, Trade and commerce	Memory loss, Unable to process information methodically, Ego makes them communicate in unfriendly manner, Erratic decision making while doing business.
Venus	Love, Beauty, Luxury, Romance, Marriage, Sex, Partnerships	Pride and ego in relationships causes it to break, Marry for money and prestige, Want luxurious properties and conveyances resulting in high levels of stress.
Mars	Fire, Energy, Action, Electricity, Military, Blood, Security	Power hungry, Indulge in fights and wars due to emotional hurt, Danger of fire, accidents, and thefts. Property disputes.
Jupiter	Religion and God, Philosophy, Banking and Finance, Ministers and Advisors	Rates himself highly knowledgeable in of like a know it all. Very proud. Can be virtuous but indulges in hype and loses direction. Affects judgment and decision making ability.
Saturn	Common man, Labor class, Servants	Challenges authority and elders at home. Rude towards working class and servants and are stressed because of them. Obstruction in professional life. Have to toil a lot. Loss of prestige and honour.

The above set of results are generic and can vary based on the sign and house where the combust planet and Sun are situated. If the Sun is powerful in the horoscope and the concerned planet is influential, then the results are intensified but if the Sun is weak then the impact of the combustion is relatively benign.

A combust planet which is exalted and in good dignity will try its best to minimize adverse results.

Profound effects of combust planets or asta graha can be felt when the planet in question is within 3°20′ degree orbit to the Sun. This is the span of one Navamsha which means the combust planet gets too close to Sun for comfort.

Another point to be noted is that during combustion if the degree of the Sun is lesser than the combust planet, then the impact is said to be benign when compared to the case where the degree of the combust planet is less than the Sun. This is because in the latter, the combust planet is moving towards the Sun and is about to get eclipsed by the Sun's rays, while in the former, it is moving away from the Sun, meaning it is gradually getting out of the combustion zone.

Sun = 134°, Venus = 130° impacts Venus more seriously when compared to Sun = 134°, Venus = 138°

Combust Moon :

The planet of Moon is combust when it is within an angular distance of 12° from the Sun. This happens on the day of Amavasya and Shukla Pratipada, both of which occur every month. Thus, Moon is combust about 7% of the time or 7% of the world's population will have a combust Moon in their birth chart. Moon is the significator of the mind and the heart so a combust Moon is known to give an ambivalent and unstable mind. Decision making is either flawed or delayed or very rash.

Table No. 9: Impact of Combust Moon in various Rashis and Bhavas:

Rashi	Results	House (Bhava)	Results
Mesha	Sun is exalted here and influences the Moon. Can give fame, wealth and position of authority but irrationality creeps in.	1st	Could suffer with regards to both parents. Sun influences the Moon here.
Vrishaba	Moon is exalted here. Combustion not very intense here as Sun is weaker in sign of Venus. Native can be an artist, writer or poet.	2nd	Impacts family life adversely. Could be wealthy but is accused of wrongdoing.
Mithuna	Sign of Mercury. Native likes to run his own business related to beauty products or chemicals.	3rd	Overly courageous leading to quarrels. Wants to take risks but is scared of outcome.
Kataka	Moon's own sign which negates the impact the Sun to an extent. Native likes to indulge softer vocations including painting, singing, teaching, and also banking. Can also be a sailor or mariner.	4th	Digbala for Moon. Relatively stable. Trouble with properties and coastal areas.
Simha	Sun's sign Leo. Native wants to be a leader and likes to take up activities in the field of travel, entertainment, administration, and writing. Can trouble marriage and health.	5th	Sun negatively affects creativity and children. Troubled thoughts.

Kanya	House of Mercury. Moon even if combust indicates a quick witted trader and businessman. Can be a voice artist or into mimicry. Can also shine as a sportsman and as an actor.	6th	This can be a blessing in disguise in dealing with people with tact and diplomacy. Needs to take good care of health.
Tula	Sun is debilitated. Hence combustion likely to have minimal or no impact. Can make native quite popular with opposite sex and give a flair for anything glamorous (cinema, travel, hospitality)	7th	Issues with opposite sex. Cheating business partners. Trouble in foreign lands.
Vrischika	Moon is debilitated. Loses its entire strength under combustion. But Sun in house of friend Mars makes the native a skilled warrior or law enforcement officer lacking thought and clarity.	8th	Moon's weak here. Can affect longevity. Keeps poor health. Blood related disorders.
Dhanu	Most benign placement for combustion. Sun and Moon are comfortable here. May not be able to put forward his thoughts cogently. Can be a translator or a guide. Likes to be spiritual but Moon makes him feel ambivalent. Travels to faraway lands.	9th	Average placement. Some trouble with father figure. Wants to travel the world.

Makara	House of Saturn. Bad for both Sun and Moon alike. Takes one to foreign land. Wants to marry into luxury and comforts.	10th	Digbala for Sun. If Moon in decent dignity, native makes for a good artist, singer, poet, sea trader, pharmacist or agriculturist. Craves for public attention and appeal.
Kumbha	Can become an occultist. Wanderer. Seeks company of powerful friends.	11th	Tried to gain through network of friends. Might have many unions with opposite sex.
Meena	Tries to resolve disputes. Arbiter. Judge. Last sign. Good for sea journeys.	12th	Bad for both. Lost and aimless. Wandering. Tries to solve problems instinctively without going through the process.

Example 10:

	Mercury	Sun Moon (C)	Venus
Ketu			Asc
Mars			Rahu
	Jupiter (R)	Saturn (R)	

The above is the birth chart of a famous and controversial politician of 20th century India who served as a 5 time chief minister of his state. The native is Kataka lagna with lagna lord Moon combust (Note the 'C' in brackets) and exalted in the 11th house along with Sun. Combust but exalted Moon meant the native had a great flair for arts and literature and built upon this ability to turn himself into a successful scriptwriter in regional cinema. This acted as a launchpad for a career in public life. Jupiter's aspect on the Sun and Moon only helped him is this regard. 3rd lord Mercury placed in the 10th house meant he had great oratorical skills which he leveraged to become a highly successful politician. His first marriage which occurred during the period of Rahu dasha Sun bhukti and ultimately resulted in the death of his wife. This horoscope is afflicted by mangal dosh. He became chief minister of his state during the period of Saturn dasha Mercury bhukti. Saturn's mutual aspect with Mercury and aspect on 10th house along with it being retrograde made him a shrewd politician. He was very popular with the masses. Though in and out of power, he became a significant player in national politics. Combust Moon in the 11th house meant he gained massively through his network of acquaintances and co-workers, gaining leadership role in public life.

Combust Mercury :

Mercury is combust when it is within an angular distance of 14° from the Sun while in direct motion and within an angular distance of 12° from the Sun while in retrograde motion. Mercury always stays close to the Sun and is combust for approximately 180 days in a year. About 50% of the world's population has combust Mercury in its horoscope. As it is the planet closest to the Sun in the solar system, it being combust has relatively lesser impact when compared to other planets but as the significator of intelligence, speech and communication it can make these attributes in human beings turn awry. Such natives are often criticized for being unfriendly or taciturn when in reality they may possess a warm disposition. The mind is filled with a wide variety of random thoughts at the same time, making it difficult for them to take a refined decision.

Table No. 10: Impact of Combust Mercury in various Rashis and Bhavas:

Rashi	Results	House (Bhava)	Results
Mesha	Sun is very powerful here. Can be a sportsman or athlete. Gets into conflicts with people over principles. Argumentative.	1st	Digbala for Mercury. Ideal position for executives, administrative officers and government related work. Airs views that are not popular with ruling dispensation and lands in trouble. Comes across as being arrogant. Good with investigation.
Vrishaba	More sober here. Desires creative pursuits. Can be an architect, dancer, musician or actor.	2nd	Business decisions made in a hurry could land the native in trouble financially. Acerbic tongue.
Mithuna	Mercury's own house. If in good dignity, it can make the native a marketing professional or a writer or publisher. Thoughts will be abstract. Caters to a clique. Can have more than one marriage. Makes for a successful journalist.	3rd	More courageous and willing to take risks as Sun gets better positional strength. Good for sportsman. Prefers mechanical tasks.
Kataka	Moon's house. Native can become a designer, singer, instrumental musician or even a successful poet. Communication with opposite sex can be flawed. It also makes the native a wanderer.	4th	Absence of mother or mother plays huge role. Native can get very emotional or may build a wall around himself to not let anyone know of his private life. Aims for perfection.

Simha	Sun's own house. Will want to be authoritative and as a result fights with established order. Sharp tongue. Rash decisions based on principles land him in trouble. Can be a politician, judge or even an administrative officer.	5th	Native may be creative and have several hobbies but might not be able to express it. Can suffer losses in stock and metal markets. Very intuitive.
Kanya	Mercury exalted. Can choose any profession connected to the masses such as cinema, politics, sports or tech entrepreneur. Good at marketing and communicating but indulges in play of words to put forth his point of view. Can also be an astrologer, occultist or palmist.	6th	Native makes enemies through loose talk. Needs to think through before talking in public. If Mercury afflicted, makes him a loaner.
Tula	Sun is debilitated and thus weak. Combustion has lesser impact. Connection with foreigners. May settle abroad or marry abroad. Spouse is beneficial. Benefits through partnerships from long distance journeys. Take care of health.	7th	Quarrels in marriage and business partnerships. Lacks understanding with the partner. Sun and Mercury are both uncomfortable in the 7th house. Awkward socially.
Vrischika	Combust Mercury results in native becoming a financial analyst or banking or stock market professionals. May be burdened with litigations and court cases. Prefers foreign locations.	8th	Could have lack of happiness in marriage, problems in inheritance of properties of loss in investment on properties.

Dhanu	Can be a legal luminary, law officer or judge. Good for high positions in government. May have more than one marriage.	9th	Tries to take too many decisions in a short span of time leading to unwanted mistakes. Philosopher but questions people on their views.
Makara	Connected to armed forces mainly the air force. More into administration and government, law enforcement and investigation. If afflicted, can indulge in criminal activities.	10th	Combust Mercury makes the native take cut corners to rise to the top in profession. Loves authority but is not willing to share with others.
Kumbha	Wants a big network of friends and acquaintances that can do his bidding. Good for advertising. Finds communicating at times to be very difficult.	11th	Success comes later in life. Prefers to lead a group than be follower. Has a refined taste for finer things in life.
Meena	Mercury debilitated and already weak. Combustion weakens it further. Prefers non-verbal communication. Creative in an unconventional sort of way. Again can be a singer, dancer, painter or designer. Abstract thoughts.	12th	Wanders in foreign lands. Losses can be huge. Natural debilitation sign for Mercury. Prefers to communicate in signs or telepathically. Has his legions of admirers and detractors.

Example 11:

Jupiter (R)	Saturn (R) Ketu		
Mars			Asc Sun Mercury (C)
		Rahu	Venus (C) Moon

The native of the above chart is an economist turned politician. Lagna lord Sun is placed in the lagna itself in Simha rashi along with combust Mercury. The native is not known to mince his words and is very blunt. This has attracted many admirers but several detractors as well in public life. Mercury being combust in the 1st house but in Simha rashi means that the native has been very close to the seat of power for long periods in his life but has challenged the establishment even if they belong to the same ideology if he believes they are not in accordance with principles of fair play and justice. He loves authority yet at the same time has taken up causes which seem impossible and using his intellect cum legal acumen he has won many battles. Infact this was also the reason for his entry into politics which occurred during the period of Jupiter dasha Mercury bhukti when he got nominated as a member of parliament by the then principal opposition party of the country. Mercury here has a lower longitude (21 degrees) than that of Sun (28 degrees) and despite the powerful placement of the latter, his airing of views on several issues has not gone down well with a section of the polity, resulting in him not attaining the levels of success in politics that he could have.

Combust Venus:

Venus turns combust when it is within 10° from the Sun while in direct motion and within an angular distance of 8° from the Sun while in retrograde motion. Depending on the direction of its motion, Venus can turn combust anywhere between 5 and 80 days at a stretch during a particular year and converges to an average of 50 days in a year, when it is combust, over a decade. Venus is the planet of relationships, romance, beauty and entertainment and so when it turns combust, the light or spark in these activities goes out. You will see a lot of breakups during the time when Venus is combust. In fact, it is a fairly common advice among astrologers not to conduct a wedding when Venus is combust. The Sun's rays burn out the merriment or joy that Venus can bring about.

Table No. 11: Impact of Combust Venus in various Rashis and Bhavas:

Rashi	Results	House (Bhava)	Results
Mesha	Sun is exalted and dominates Venus here. Native might be a law enforcement or administrative service officer but will connect himself to a glamour field such as information and broadcasting. Problems in marriage.	1st	Relatively benign here as Sun is stronger in 1st house compared to Venus. People can brand you as being uncaring, dominating and inflexible.
Vrishaba	Sign of Venus. Native will try and earn plenty of wealth and fame through acting, singing, dancing or trading in luxury goods. Tries to marry into wealth.	2nd	Focus on material comforts, properties and conveyances leads to disputes with family and co-workers. Communicating plans heads up can make you avoid problems.

Mithuna	Tries to settle abroad. Better gains in foreign lands. Might be into movie production or runs entertainment channels on television. Could also be a jeweler. Multiple marriages a possibility. Changes profession often.	3rd	Courageous and loves to take risks in professional and personal life without consulting or taking proper advice. This lands the individual in trouble but also gives unprecedented success.
Kataka	Gets popular because of females but can turn hostile. Wants to take leadership position in relationships and bring about change in his profession. Emotionally driven.	4th	Digbala for Venus. Craves for luxury in life. Wants to invest in property in prime locations but lands him into trouble.
Simha	Sun's own house. Might be a fashion designer, textile or diamond merchant. Leads industrial houses. Gets bossy and arrogant towards subordinates and wife.	5th	Entertainer. Gambles in casinos and card games. Can make a name for himself through such professions but might incur huge losses.
Kanya	Venus is debilitated here. Marriage can be unconventional. Lack of communication can break relationships. Better to take up Sun related vocations connected to the government. Financial losses are likely with his combination.	6th	Financial stress. Heavy burden of loans. Disputes with banks and in-laws. Trouble with authorities.

Tula	House of Venus. Sun is debilitated here, so Venus becomes more powerful here. Marriage can bring hidden benefits. Connected to hospitality, travel or airline industry or even an architect.	7th	Indicates the native may have relationship with multiple women. Often changes his business plans without giving it much thought.
Vrischika	Venus feels uncomfortable in house of Mars and gets burnt by the Sun. But this is an intuitive sign and thus native can become a tantric or astrologer. Can host talk shows on television or internet and gain fame. Needs to be careful with finances.	8th	Sudden inheritance but this land him into a court case. Joint finances can result in losses because of poor planning.
Dhanu	Might marry into wealth. Wife can bring fortune and success. Native might be an educationist, judge, or connected to law enforcement or a techie. Wants to travel the world. Has good intuition. Multiple marriages possible. Spouse may be a foreigner or from another culture.	9th	Religious but curious to know about other faiths. Spouse can be met through long distance journeys or at a place of higher learning.
Makara	Can be a doctor, scientist, engineer or IT professional. Marries a woman or status. Might be an interior designer or architect. Needs to learn to co-operate with spouse.	10th	Craves for attention. Chooses a profession connected to glamour or the masses. Loves to be an influencer.

Kumbha	Loves authority and a large network of friends and admirers. Likes to delegate work. Ideal for higher posts in government. Business may be beset with problems if decisions taken without much thought.	11th	Leverages of his friends circle and gains through them. Can become an audio/video influencer or even an author.
Meena	Venus exalted. May marry to settle abroad. Is a born artist but has to work hard to prove his talent. Could be a legendary singer or actor. Wants to take center stage.	12th	Prefers to live abroad. Tries to cut corners to get to the top of his profession.

Example 12:

	Rahu		
Jupiter			
Mercury Venus (C) Sun	Saturn	Asc Moon Ketu Mars	

Above horoscope is that of a leading actress in the Bollywood industry. She has Tula lagna with lagna lord Venus combust and placed in the 3rd house along with Sun and Mercury. Moon's ownership of the 10th house and its placement in the 1st house meant that she always wanted to associate herself to a profession connected to the glamour world. Combust Venus placed in the 3rd house in Dhanu rashi has meant that she had the intuition and courage to choose roles in movies that would bring her into prominence and expand her repertoire. She made her debut in the Hindi film industry in the period of Jupiter dasha Saturn bhukti and has had a successful innings so far. Rahu's placement in the seventh house and combust Venus in the 3rd house meant she chose a life partner outside of her community and married him during the period of Jupiter dasha Rahu bhukti.

Combust Mars:

Mars goes combust when it is within 17° from the Sun. Unlike Mercury and Venus, Mars, Jupiter and Saturn can never be retrograde and combust at the same time. (Recall from the section on retrograde planets that Mars, Jupiter and Saturn retrograde when they are placed anywhere between the 5th to 8th sign from the Sun while the theory of combustion works on the principle of planets in close proximity to the Sun). Mars goes combust once every two years for a period of anywhere between 90 and 120 days. Approximately 15% of the world's population has a combust Mars in its horoscope. Mars is the planet of action, war, conflicts, risk taking and physical activities. Thus a Mars combust in your horoscope could result in you challenging and fighting elected authorities, engaging in petty conflicts or clashes, indulging in crimes, thefts or robberies. This may be for a noble cause but things might get out of hand which could land you in trouble. Fire accidents, blasts or property disputes are also indicated by a combust Mars.

Table No. 12: Impact of Combust Mars in various Rashis and Bhavas:

Rashi	Results	House (Bhava)	Results
Mesha	Exalted Sun in the house of Mars indicates stormy nature. A great placement for a sportsman or an athlete. Native will be a born leader of men. Domineering, boastful and arrogant. Needs to be careful with finances because of rash nature.	1st	Powerful for Sun and Mars. President or Prime minister of his country. Industrialist, Captain in team sports. Fire accidents possible.
Vrishaba	Attracted to everything foreign. May settle abroad. Could find life partner there. Needs to be careful not to get attracted to drugs as they may lead to chaos in life. Good placement for interior designers.	2nd	Vituperative speech lands him in trouble. Rash with investments. Focuses too much on owning properties.
Mithuna	May be connected to telecom department of the government. Could marry a wealthy man or woman. Administrative officer, judge or army officer. Powerful political orator.	3rd	Upachaya. Better results after the age of 30. Loves taking risks. Combative nature. Overbearing on communication. Action oriented.
Kataka	Mars debilitated and weak. Sun dominates here. Associated with politics or government but may be riddled with corruption charges. May be out of power or in the dark for longer periods of time.	4th	Loses in wars or conflicts especially on home turf. Lacks happiness. Mind is full of worries. Needs to be careful while traveling on road, rail and sea journeys.

Simha	Sun's own house. Military commander, surgeon, sportsman or an intelligence officer. Highly competitive but lack of empathy gets him into conflicts in both professional and personal life. Loves the limelight. Good for actors. Loves animation and graphics.	5th	Harsh with children. Probably wants to teach them practical lessons of life. Too much seriousness prevents him from enjoying life.
Kanya	Possesses psychic abilities. Strong intuition. Beset with health problems. Quarrels with people. If controlled, can become a motivational speaker, spiritual guru, numerologist or vastu expert.	6th	Lots of enemies in life. Partially successful in quest to defeat them. Loses patience too sun.
Tula	Sun debilitated here and is weak. House of Venus. Issues in relationship but if ironed out can give lot of benefits. May attract favors from opposite sex. Could be a financial analyst, banker or revenue officer.	7th	Could be a military dictator. Fights with partners over results and their decision making abilities. Mangal dosh.
Vrischika	House of Mars. Might marry a doctor. May be a navy or air force officer. Attracts court cases and litigations.	8th	Mangal dosh. Strong sex drive. Pugnacious. Disputes over land belonging to ancestors. Partner's life span comes into question.

Dhanu	Fiery by nature. Could be neo-philosopher who establishes own dharma and religious order in a foreign land challenging authority in his native land. Could marry abroad and settle down there permanently but problems in marriage. Spiritual.	9th	Challenges religious authorities. May convert to prove his point of view. Danger of accidents during journey by sea.
Makara	Mars exalted. Combustion has lesser impact. Still native likes to lead a business empire connected to the field of medical profession, pharma, big technology, oil & gas. Could be a senior government official. Sportsman.	10th	Digbala for Mars. Will always want to be boss and never work under anyone. Leads to tempestuous clashes.
Kumbha	Engineer, scientist, software developer. Problems with the masses.	11th	Chases after wealth and comforts. May succeed with respect to chemical and hazardous equipment.
Meena	Water sign owned by Jupiter. Wanderlust. Connected to travel or hospitality industry. Could be an event manager. Desires increased ownership and control but may have problems with the partner.	12th	Not good for Mars and Sun. Lands into trouble in foreign countries. Tries to force others to accept his perspectives in group discussions. Loses friends as a result.

Example 13:

	Moon	Saturn	Asc Venus
			Ketu Mercury
Rahu			Sun Mars (C)
Jupiter			

Example 13 is the birth chart of a versatile and highly successful Hollywood actress. Lagna lord is Mercury and is placed in the 2nd house of Moon with Venus posited in the lagna, all of which are combinations of professions connected to glamour, communication, creativity and entertainment. Native has Mars combust in 3rd house conjunct with Sun which gave her a flair to be in the limelight. This placement made her a highly courageous individual willing to take risks and follow the road less traveled. She entered the world of modeling in the early 1990's during the mahadasha of Mars and before the mahadasha ended, she got her first offer in Hollywood in the comedy genre which turned out to be a big success. She has never looked back, carving out a niche for herself in the action genre playing a number of characters in movies where she is seen bashing the bad guys.

Combust Jupiter :

Jupiter goes combust when it is within 11° from the Sun. Like Mars, Jupiter can never be retrograde and combust at the same time. Jupiter goes combust once every year for a period of 30 days. Approximately 8% of the world's population has a combust Jupiter in its horoscope. Jupiter is the planet that is known to impart knowledge and wisdom. It is the planet of spirituality, religion, philosophy, higher learning and dharma. When Jupiter turns combust, it makes the native boastful and proud of himself especially with regards to his knowledge and talents. In the process, he loses sight of the goal leading to unfavorable outcomes. His ability to judge situations, people and places also get compromised. He tends to overhype the state of affairs based on his expertise and some secret or additional information he may be privy to. Such a native feels that other people should shower him with praises for his abilities. Ego clashes lead to trouble with ministers and people of higher authorities.

Table No. 13: Impact of Combust Jupiter in various Rashis and Bhavas:

Rashi	Results	House (Bhava)	Results
Mesha	Exalted Sun is powerful here. Jupiter in house of its friend Mars. Native can be a jurist or legal luminary but tends to be a show off. Also good for armed forces. Could be an engineer connected to the military. Minister in government. Very competitive in nature. Sportsman. Marriage generally not an issue unless native tends to dominate wife.	1st	Digbala for Jupiter. Religious but dogmatic. Tries to push through his ideology even if there are no takers. If Jupiter not afflicted can lead an army of men or have a military commander status like in society. Could be a famed industrialist.
Vrishaba	Tends to settle abroad. Likes to be creative. Fashion designer, Graphic designer or Video gamer. Entrepreneurial by nature.	2nd	Wants his family to follow his principles in accordance with traditions. Could be stingy and miserly.

Mithuna	Consultant. Journalist. Owner of television, print or digital media platform. Loves to lead from the front. Good for entrepreneurship. Craves for high status in society. Educationist. Tech crazy.	3rd	Communicative but boastful about his knowledge. Might be virtuous but needs to respect other people's views. Can try to be a successful sportsperson. Should practice yoga and meditation to maintain a balanced lifestyle.
Kataka	Exalted Jupiter so not much of a problem. Has strong views on family life and spouse. Authoritative. Could be connected to the fine arts and music. Loves designing and creating apps.	4th	Needs to be accommodating of his colleagues. Tends to take things to the heart if he is not praised and criticized. Investments to be made after careful examination of property.
Simha	Sun's own house. Leadership material. Politician, Administrative officer, Judge or even an educationist. Indulges in stock markets and gold trading. Loves contesting and winning elections.	5th	Tries to choose career for children and boss them around. Needs to be hands-off and allow offspring to follow their dreams. Taking up a hobby like music can help.
Kanya	May marry a woman of a foreign country. Could be a talented sportsperson or a skilled engineer. May have multiple sources of income and frequent changes in professional life.	6th	This is a good placement for politicians and IAS officers. Such individuals are unbending and lose friends as a result.

Tula	Sun is debilitated and weak. Jupiter in house of Venus is not so comfortable. May ask for too much beauty in wife. May achieve success as a beautician, makeup artist or hair dresser. Health setbacks indicated.	7th	Tries to compete with spouse on matters of religion, knowledge and philosophy. Also in matters of commerce, native doesn't like taking orders from colleagues or partners.
Vrischika	Good for scientific researcher, AI professional, software developer, security analyst, intelligence bureau professional. May marry someone from same profession. Stresses out too often.	8th	Can have a long life. If not afflicted, native can become an investigative journalist or an intelligence bureau or secret service officer. Needs to learn to co-operate with others. Can be a financial analyst. Could make for an astrologer, tantric or a spiritual guru. Causes health issues.
Dhanu	Could be a banker or financial services professional. Connected to law and legal system. Judge or seasoned and successful lawyer. Meets spouse in foreign lands. May settle there. Multiple marriages a possibility.	9th	Travels to foreign lands and engages in discourse on a wide variety of topics. Can be highly educated but needs to use his knowledge and skill set for the betterment of society. Scientist and innovator.

Makara	Jupiter is debilitated and uncomfortable here. Loss of wealth or obstacles in wealth accumulation. Better to hold a government related job than run your own business or be involved in the private sector.	10th	Success after disputes at the workplace. Tends to not respect co-workers. Health issues on account of stress. Better to go for a government job.
Kumbha	May be a jeweler or a gold trader. Spouse may hold a high position in the government. Could be connected to the oil & gas industry. Scientist. Problems with health as you age.	11th	Better here. Gains after the age of 30 after facing a lot of obstacles. Could be connected to media or entertainment business or even be a civil servant. Research oriented.
Meena	Doctor, Engineer, Lawyer, Educationist, Police officer or even a banking professional. Lives abroad. Could splurge his wealth on costly and unwanted materials. Financial setbacks. Detached by nature.	12th	Runs a charitable trust, yoga school or an ashram. Exercises strict control over surroundings. Can have many followers. Can be successful in foreign lands after facing failures first.

Example 14:

Moon		Ketu	Venus
Mars (R)			Asc
			Sun Jupiter (C)
	Saturn Rahu		Mercury

Above is the birth chart of a well-known politician of India. She has her lagna lord Moon placed in the 9th house in Meena rashi. Jupiter is combust in the 2nd house with Sun and is aspect by Mars. This combination made her develop a combative nature and leadership abilities from a young age, qualities which have helped her have a long innings in public life despite a number of adversaries. She has contested and won a number of elections. She has also been a hands-on mother to her son and nursed his career in his initial days in the political arena.

Combust Saturn:

Saturn goes combust when it is within 15° from the Sun. Like Mars and Jupiter, Saturn can never be retrograde and combust at the same time. Saturn goes combust once every year for a period of 36 days which means that about 10% of the world's population has a combust Saturn in its horoscope. Saturn is the planet of restrictions, sorrows, misfortune, delays and setbacks. It is a hard taskmaster and likes to impart discipline and orderliness, words which are not palatable to many human beings. It is also known that Saturn and Sun are natural enemies (Saturn is the son of Sun and is known as Chhayaputra). Any conjunction of the Sun and Saturn is known to cause obstructions in both professional and personal life, more so if Saturn becomes combust. Combust Saturn can make the native harsh, rude, disobedient both towards the elders in his family as well as his bosses and co-workers. Saturn is the planet of the aam aadmi or common man as a result of which such natives may venture into public life or politics. Still they may be disrespectful and condescending towards the working class and lower strata of the society. This placement also makes the native work very hard if he or she wants to climb the ladder of success in life. Disappointments and setbacks are many.

These people are born rebels challenging cherished traditions and leadership at every step.

Table No. 14: Impact of Combust Saturn in various Rashis and Bhavas:

Rashi	Results	House (Bhava)	Results
Mesha	Saturn is debilitated and weak while Sun is exalted and strong. Neechabanga raja yoga. Can bless native with high authority in the armed forces. Can be a powerful military commander or politician. Results are mixed though. Marriage after careful deliberation.	1st	Slow mover. Doesn't enjoy the finer aspects of life. Timid. Doesn't enjoy the company of many human beings. Could be a loner.
Vrishaba	Better for Saturn. Can bless native with luxuries through opposite sex. Tries to marry into wealth. Native is a movie director, writer, actor or dancer capable of influencing the masses. Chases after material comforts.	2nd	Obstacles in wealth accumulation. Faulty investments may hinder him. Takes time opening up to people. Not very brave compared to other positions.
Mithuna	Marries a foreigner or settles in a foreign or faraway land connected to the spouse. Professional writer. Can achieve worldwide acclaim. Changes jobs too often. Needs to be careful not to quarrel with spouse or marriage can fall apart.	3rd	Aggressive. Gradually takes risks as he grows in life. Learns to communicate by observing others. Can serve as an assistant to a powerful leader.

Kataka	Loves and craves authority and power for himself. Connected to the government. Politician. Can also be a navy or air force officer. Mental health setbacks.	4th	Property particularly by the coast, facing the west direction lead to court disputes. Could have issues on account of mother or mother land. Prefers to live abroad.
Simha	Slightly more creative here. Can be an engineer, IT professional or software developer or even a doctor. Wealthy after initial setbacks. Needs to be careful of fire.	5th	Too strict and disciplined as a result loses out on creativity and merriment. Needs to cool off. Expects his children to follow in his footsteps. Potential problems with childbirth.
Kanya	Could be an architect, singer, actor, director, debater or even a journalist. Works very hard to achieve lead roles in cinemas and gains iconic status. Can have multiples marriages. Chases after money, property and other creature comforts. Keeps poor health.	6th	Warrior like. Fights with bosses as well as sub-ordinates. Borrows heavily and gets in to trouble but if careful can make handsome gains. High mental stress levels leads to breakdown. Has to work very hard in life to achieve success.
Tula	Saturn exalted while Sun is debilitated. Neechabanga raja yoga. Results are dictated more by Saturn. Native becomes an actor, director, scriptwriter or musician of great repute in mainstream cinema. Can also become a successful fashion, dress or costume designer. Native may get married late in life.	7th	Marriage gets delayed. If he takes rash decisions, may lead to unhappy conjugal life. Stormy clashes with business associates indicated.

Vrischika	Administrative or police officer or even a government spy. Loves politics and government related work. Could also be an air force officer. Achieves highest rank in service. Separation in marriage is indicated.	8th	Long life span but sudden and tense end. Be careful while traveling by road. Accident prone. Investment disputes. Sudden occurrences in life. Can have issues with in-laws.
Dhanu	Could be connected to the hospitality or travel related industry. Might be connected to the transport department in the government. Associated with the banking and financial services industry.	9th	Changes religion or inter-religious marriage. Can be well educated but this knowledge often leads to disputes with people of different ideology.
Makara	Saturn's own house. Mountain climber like a goat. Physical trainer, gym instructor or a yoga master. Connected to the fitness industry. Could train celebrity artists or sportspersons. Could be connected to the petroleum or Iron industry. Success after the age of 36.	10th	Obstacles at each step of professional life. A number of adversaries. As a result person can be very combative or very innovative.
Kumbha	May be connected to airline, hotel or travel industry. Has a large network of friends and acquaintances. This placement could make you a bold and successful businessman.	11th	Better placement. Will make steady gains in life post the age of 30 after facing failures initially in life. Likes a large network of friends cutting across different sections of the society. May have a number of admirers among the downtrodden.

Meena	Lives in foreign lands. Again associates himself with travel, airline or event management industries. Could even be an aerospace engineer or a pilot. Scientific and inquisitive nature. Mind is always filled with deep thoughts. Loves traveling. Marries outside the community. Could have multiple marriages.	12th	Many losses. Wanders in foreign lands. Inter-caste marriage. Lives among the poor but fights for their rights.

Example 15:

Sun Mercury (C) Saturn (C) Venus			Asc
Jupiter			Ketu
Mars Rahu			
	Moon		

Native was a world famous scientist who propounded the theory of relativity. Lagna lord Mercury is combust in 10th house in Meena rashi. This house has 4 planets with Saturn also combust here. Native was known to be inquisitive from a young age and even dropped out of school rebelling against the policy of rote learning. He published more than 300 scientific papers and inspired path breaking development in the fields of physics and quantum theory but had his fair share of intellectual disputes with leading scientist of the time. Note the Saturn being combust with Mercury and Sun in Meena rashi indicates native doesn't easily believe in existing theories and tries to push the boundaries of scientific reasoning. He married twice and was linked to other women as well. Native had to migrate to the US because of his Jewish background during the 1930s.

Chapter 4

Planetary Conjunctions

In the previous chapter, we examined the impact of planets in a state of combustion. This occurs on account of these planets being in close proximity to the Sun. An old English proverb often used in modern times is that a man is known by the company he keeps. This holds good for planets as well as well. After all, it is natural for any entity to be influenced by its surroundings.

When two or more planets are in close proximity or conjunct each other, each of these planets is influenced by the other and the result that it provides gets altered by the companionship of the planets it is in close proximity to. The results will naturally vary based on the sign and house that the planets are placed in. Other factors to consider include the lagna of the native, placement of the planets concerned in the Navamsha and how deep the conjunction is (Longitude of the said planets in the house).

In this chapter, we will study the impact of conjunction of two planets in various houses starting with conjunctions of Moon. For the sake of simplicity, we will exclude the lunar nodes, Rahu and Ketu from this study.

Conjunctions of Moon:

1. Mars: Moon is soft while Mars is hard. Moon is feminine while Mars is masculine. Moon is watery while Mars is fiery.

Yet when they combine, the calming influence of Moon coupled with the relentless energy of Mars gives rise to a raja yoga known as Chandra Mangala Yoga. The soft Moon and the rash Mars which are known to be friends bless the native who has such a placement with wealth, property, conveyances and luxurious lifestyle. Money is never a problem for such people. On the flipside, such natives can be harsh with their mothers. Natives with Chandra Mangala yoga are known for their candor, courage and diplomacy. They may gain from alloys, spirits and things made of clay or leather. At the same time this combination is known to cause poor circulation of blood.

Table No. 15: Conjunction of Moon and Mars:

House (Bhava)	Results
1st	Native is short tempered. Attains a high position in society especially in professional life. Can suffer from disorders pertaining to blood. Is also prone to fire accidents or injuries to the head.
2nd	This is a very good placement for wealth accumulation but native here is devoid of good relations at home and is often stressed. Criticized for airing his views.
3rd	Native tends to be very aggressive at times. Can be a wealthy and famous sportsman. Is accident prone. Needs to be careful while traveling by road.
4th	Native is restless and lacks peace of mind. Quarrels at home and problems with mother. Wealthy and propertied individual but lots of obstacles and enmity on account of the same wealth. Bad for sons.
5th	This is an excellent placement for getting all the riches of life. Native can be a highly successful businessman if blessing of Jupiter is present. Gets success through speculation.

6th	Suffers from diseases of the mind. Has a number of enemies and obstacles in life. Is poor and devoid of good relations with the mother or the mother doesn't live long. This placement can however give extraordinary results post the age of 30 as it is an upachaya house.
7th	Seeks other people's wealth. Speaks a lot but is not truthful. Marital discord particularly on account of in-laws. Mangal dosha can affect peaceful atmosphere at home.
8th	Dushtasthana house. Can result in marital discord and land disputes with extended family. Needs to be careful on voyages by sea. Sudden occurrences are many.
9th	Great placement for a long, wealthy and highly prosperous life. Native succeeds more in foreign lands. Could be a banker or lawyer. Very spiritual and philosophical.
10th	Best placement for this combination. Native holds a position of prestige in the land of his birth. He is very valorous, wealthy and his blessed with many properties, conveyance and all other types of riches. Connected with government and administration.
11th	As good as the placement in the 10th house. Native could become exceedingly wealthy like an emperor. Blessed with all luxuries of life, a good family and number of friends across all walks of life. Very popular with opposite sex.
12th	Probably the worst placement for this conjunction. Native is wither poor or loses his wealth through either deceit, speculation or a major legal dispute. Lives in faraway lands. Many problems at home. Diseases related to the bile.

2. Mercury: Moon represents our emotions while Mercury represents our intellect. Both planets also represent the speed and execution of our thoughts and thus have a direct bearing on our actions. A favorable conjunction of these two planets can make the native a highly religious and learned individual complete possessing a repertoire of skills. Such an individual is likely to be a scholar with a literary or artistic mindset. He has a smiling face, is affable and is likely to be very popular with the opposite sex. He is soft spoken, leads a wealthy and prosperous life and becomes famous.

Table No. 16: Conjunction of Moon and Mercury:

House (Bhava)	Results
1st	Native has a sharp mind and is blessed with mental and physical stamina. He is attractive, eloquent and is praised for his work.
2nd	Wealth is accumulated with some effort. Blessed with good family life. Is liberal minded and jocular.
3rd	Poetic by nature. Loves to engage in conversation and debates. Could turn that into his profession. Maybe a journalist if 10th house matters support the birth chart.
4th	Attractive appearance. Native is wealthy and is blessed with land, property and conveyances. He also has good children and a number of friends.
5th	Favorable placement for children. They may become authors or artists. Good placement for doing business connected with big tech and water related activities. Lucky in romance. Native is poetic.
6th	This is one placement where native's speech can get him into trouble. People with such combination are always tense and suffer from anxiety disorder. Upachaya house as a result of which native can attain great heights post the age of 30 because of his work especially if Jupiter is aspecting this combination.
7th	Native can be poet, author or a scriptwriter. He has a great aesthetic sense. Good placement for businessman. Native can attain a very high position in society. Gets a beautiful wife.
8th	Longevity maybe an issue unless Jupiter or Saturn are involved. Poor investment decisions could land him in trouble.
9th	Is a philosopher by nature. Prefers to live in faraway land and travel extensively. Accumulates wealth steadily. Blessed with good children. Courageous and a risk taker.
10th	Native is wealthy and famous. He rises to a high position in society but can suffer from poor relations with his family. Maybe a voyageur. Prefers to live in coastal areas.

11th	All round gains and prosperity in life. Wealthy and learned. Positive developments after the age of 30. Popular with the opposite sex. May have many relations.
12th	Poor. Indolent and lazy. Great literary tastes but is criticized for his opinions even if they are correct. Stays unhappy.

3. Jupiter: The conjunction of Moon and Jupiter is a famous one in Vedic astrology and leads to the renowned and much talked about raja yoga known as Gaja Kesari yoga. Jupiter is the planet for wealth, knowledge, fame, luck and children while Moon signifies the mind and the heart, happiness and prosperity. When the two planets combine, they bless the native with all types of luxuries and comforts. Gaja means Elephant which signifies luck, enormity and an unbridled quest for knowledge while Kesari meaning Lion is the epitome of courage, leadership and regality. Natives of this yoga are intelligent, knowledgeable, highly educated, wealthy and prosperous. They occupy a very high position in their profession and in the societal hierarchy. They are born leader of men and are known for their courage, tact and diplomacy and easily defeat their enemies. They are also blessed with a big and very happy family. Above all, people with Gaja Kesari yoga are remembered and praised for their achievements and contributions to humanity for centuries after their lifetime.

Table No. 17: Conjunction of Moon and Jupiter:

House (Bhava)	Results
1st	Best placement for this conjunction. Native has a soft and gentle disposition. He rises high in life and occupies and eminent position. He has a broad elevated chest and a good body. He maintains cordial relations with all and begets a good wife and sons.

2nd	Great placement for attaining riches in life. Native is soft spoken and possesses a musical voice. He is blessed with a rich and prosperous family.
3rd	Native is a renowned author or leads a publishing business. Is widely traveled. He is blessed with good brothers and sisters.
4th	Native is the owner of many luxury goods in life. He is landed, propertied and leads a comfortable and happy life. Native is intelligent, learned and rises to the position of a minister and is also endowed with happiness with regards to his relations.
5th	Native is blessed with artistic and beautiful children. He is a very intelligent businessman. Native may also be renowned in the entertainment industry.
6th	Results here are better after the age of 30. Native makes for an accomplished diplomat or an intelligence bureau officer. Solves exceedingly difficult problems for the government or elected authorities.
7th	This is a very good placement with regards to marriage. Native is blessed with a beautiful spouse with noble qualities. He makes for a very good businessman and engages in trade and commerce. He is intelligent and clever in all his dealings and is the favorite of the king.
8th	Jupiter blesses the native with a good longevity. Native may be blessed with a rich and beautiful spouse and good marital happiness. He has a soft disposition but is often tensed.
9th	Native is highly educated and very intelligent. Could be a scientist. Expert in physical sciences. Religious and well versed in the shastras and puranas. He would make for a renowned author. Travels the world.
10th	Highly successful and skilled professional administrator or businessman. He is cool-headed, good looking and very generous in giving. He is learned wealthy and commands respect in society.
11th	Abundance in wealth, knowledge and family. Most likely is an innovator. Deals in chemicals and liquid items. He is the favorite of the king and the government and is handsomely rewarded by them. Highly prosperous in life and remembered after his time.
12th	Not a great placement. Turns into a wanderer. Native however may discover or solve chronic problems in faraway lands.

4. Venus: Both Moon and Venus are watery planets and signify our aesthetic aspects of our life. Both of them also signify romance and luxuries. A native with a Moon conjunct Venus will have a natural flair for trade and merchandise particularly related to businesses such as textiles, jewellery and concoctions. He puts on fine apparel and is fond of scents and flowers. He is clever in execution of his work and is popular among his people but could at the same time be lethargic.

Table No. 18: Conjunction of Moon and Venus:

House (Bhava)	Results
1st	Native has a pleasing personality and is a favorite of his seniors. He is an expert in matters of the apparel and scents, gems and jewellery and flowers. He has association with many women.
2nd	Soft nature. Quiet and goes about his business in a workmanlike approach. Attached to the family. Wealth accumulates over a period of time.
3rd	Doesn't seek risk. Gains financially from media and entertainment. Undertakes a number of short journeys.
4th	Popular with people. Leads a luxurious life. He gains financially from ships, boats or by articles transported by or across water. He enjoys the company and gets happiness from opposite sex.
5th	Connected to fine arts. Could be an actor, singer, dancer or a director. Romantic nature. Emotional. All the world's a stage. If not afflicted, can be exceedingly wealthy.
6th	Not a great placement. Wealthy but can lack good relations with family and friends. Takes a contrarian approach.
7th	Intelligent but may fritter away his wealth. Might work as a spy for governmental organizations. Attached to women. Multiple marriages possible.
8th	This placement affects longevity unless Jupiter or Saturn is involved. Native gets sudden inheritance but could also face litigations.

9th	Gains more in foreign lands. Wealthy and respected by his friends and colleagues. Wife could be of foreign origin. Travels through the sea.
10th	Native is kind and forgiving by nature. He is surrounded by a number of people. Maybe a famous minister or king. Commands respect of his subjects. Is wealthy.
11th	Has a large network of friends particularly with regards opposite sex. Benefits through their association. Native is chivalrous and mischievous but always thinks of gains. Businesslike approach to everyday life.
12th	Gain of money from foreign lands. Loves journeys through the sea. Could be a mariner or a sea trader.

5. Saturn: Those born with a Moon-Saturn conjunction start their life with the much feared sade sati or 7.5 period of Saturn. Sade sati brings about a number of challenges resulting in the native making him feel stressed out or overwhelmed by the complexities of life. As such it is a period when the native's patience and resolve is tested and necessitates additional effort in all his undertakings. A Moon-Saturn conjunction indicates the native will have poor relations with his parents and his spouse. He will only derive unhappiness from his family. He will be devoid of wealth and be a subordinate to another. He will have liaison with women older than himself. Such an individual finds himself in controversies and gets vanquished by his opponents.

Table No. 19: Conjunction of Moon and Saturn:

House (Bhava)	Results
1st	Native is sinful, lethargic, greedy and wicked. He is rude and spends his life in a subordinate position.
2nd	Works very hard to accumulate wealth. Maybe connected to the transportation or infrastructure industries. Slow in speech and in his deeds. Family life may be a problem.

3rd	Native takes risks and accomplishes tasks in society where others fail. He is honored and respected by the government. He suffers from poor relations with his brothers.
4th	Native may be connected to the mining or petroleum industry and derives his wealth from such ventures. He accumulates land and properties through the course of his life. He may also be connected to shipping or jewelry industry. He becomes powerful and popular.
5th	Delay in birth of children but they could be highly accomplished. Lacks creativity. Associates himself with the established order and resists any change in society.
6th	Earns praise from multilateral organizations and he government in executing exceedingly difficult tasks. Earns wealth through sovereign. Devoid of good relation with in-laws. Mind is troubled with negative thoughts.
7th	Late marriage. Spouse maybe elderly or very young but very attractive. He may suffer from marital discord. He occupies a high position in his chosen profession and is honored by the government.
8th	Lifespan can be long. Obstruction in joint finances. Investments lead to heavy losses. Could be an ascetic or a psychic.
9th	Native undertakes pilgrimages or spiritual retreats to discover the true meaning of life. Develops patience and perseverance in resolving differences with his family members and professional acquaintances. Truth seeker.
10th	Tastes success after much effort. He defeats his enemies and becomes the head of a very large organization. Native is famous. He may not have good relations with his mother.
11th	Native gains through association of his friends and acquaintances. Becomes very wealthy in the latter part of his life. Could be associated with the entertainment industry.
12th	Native wanders aimlessly. Has a troubled mind and often enters into arguments with colleagues and family members. Loses all his wealth.

Conjunctions of Mars:

1. Mercury: The conjunction of Mars and Mercury is an interesting one as it combines a fiery planet with an earthly one. Both Mars and Mercury known for their quick-wittedness. Natives with such a combination in their birth chart will be enterprising and dynamic and are born diplomats. He will gain by trade and commerce. Dealings through earthly elements such as oil, plants and trees or even timber may bring about handsome gains. He will be strongly built with broad shoulders. Such a native also succeeds in dealings associated with sale of medicine, hardware machinery, arts or crafts. Native however is not wealthy and does not have a good marriage. He may have liaison with wicked women or widows. He tries to live off others money.

Table No. 20: Conjunction of Mars and Mercury:

House (Bhava)	Results
1st	Native is cruel and aggressive but very efficient in his work. He gains from articles associated with fire or in manufacturing of metal articles. Makes for a good ambassador or a secret service agent.
2nd	Native has a sharp tongue and indulges in play of words and double entendre. He makes his hobby his profession. It is difficult for him to work under someone.
3rd	Native is a diplomat or a spy. He is clever in his dealings with everyone. He is bold and has a flair for taking unprecedented risks. He may run a successful business empire with his siblings.
4th	Native has a large network of friends but is devoid of good relations with his family. He may be boycotted by them. He is wealthy and has many properties and leads a comfortable life.
5th	Native is bereft of happiness from children. Highly intelligent but his unconventional statements may land him in trouble.

6th	Native has a number of adversaries at the workplace who prevent is promotion. He takes a number of financial risks which land him in trouble. He may have blood disorders. Can overcome all problems through exercise and meditation.
7th	Native is a wanderer and gets oppressed by low people. He is very argumentative and enters into controversies. His first marriage ends prematurely.
8th	Native is diplomatic and unfriendly. He treats his subordinates in a crude manner. He is prone to injuries and accidents. May inherit property suddenly.
9th	Native is a highly accomplished engineer or computer scientist. He has a number of patents. He becomes a renowned educator.
10th	Native is bold and persevering. He is a favorite of the king or the government. He is cruel and wicked and may occupy a high position in the armed forces or a top bureaucratic post in the government.
11th	Native is successful in all his endeavors. He is a successful businessman and owns a large enterprise. He is wealthy, highly educated and has a big network of friends.
12th	Native is crafty in all his dealings. He is prone to fire accidents. He does not maintain cordial relation with his spouse or in-laws. Foreign lands may bring sudden benefits to him.

2. Jupiter: Mars and Jupiter are the best of friends and like good buddies try and help and fortify one another. Mars sees Jupiter as a guide and a guru while the latter turns to the former for leadership. Remember, Mars functions as a captain of the navagrahas. The conjunction of Mars and Jupiter in a native's horoscope makes him the mayor of a town or a high ranking minister in the government. He receives money and patronage from the king. Native will be renowned for his knowledge of shastras and astras. He will be proficient in the vedas and mathematics but will also be over-sexed. He will also be skilled in arts and crafts. Such a native will be intelligent, strong, courteous, be blessed with sons and long lived.

Table No. 21: Conjunction of Mars and Jupiter:

House (Bhava)	Results
1st	Native is an enthusiastic individual full of energy. He will have many admirable qualities and will earn fame in the religious field. He will become a minister to the king or occupy an equally eminent post.
2nd	Wealthy but lots of obstruction on the path of glory. Tries to maintain cordial relations with his family and friends. Very blunt but candid in his speech. Tries to use the same to resolve deadlocks.
3rd	Aggressive, honest and forthcoming by nature. Native may be a renowned sportsman. Gets the happiness of brothers who may be a loyal disciple of the native.
4th	Native will be a determined and persistent individual and will lead a comfortable life. He will have many friends and good relations. He will be god-fearing and honor his religious preceptors and ancestors. He will be a minister.
5th	Highly acclaimed children. Native likes to follow dharma and inculcates the same to future generations. Multi-talented but rash at times.
6th	Good position for an administrator or a minister to a king. Overcomes his enemies but does not have good relation with his family.
7th	Native will be well-traveled and will visit mountains, forests and watery places. He is courageous. He has good relations but will lack marital happiness.
8th	Long lived. Gets sudden benefits from investments. Inherits a fortune from ancestors but that could lead to legal disputes. Spouse may be good-looking but ill-tempered. Native could be an accountant, financial manager or a lawyer.
9th	Native is religious but likes to modernize his religion. He is well-versed in all ancient scriptures and wants to teach the same to the present generation. Wealthy and reputed.

10th	Native attains a kingly position and enjoys much fame. He is a highly skilled individual who is very wealthy and begets a large family.
11th	Native is very wealthy and charitable. He leads a large organization and is accomplished in the vedas and shastras.
12th	Native is prone to accidents. Is better of living in foreign lands. He is bereft of marital happiness.

3. Venus: Men are from Mars while women are from Venus. This one statement is enough to signify how poles apart Mars and Venus are. Mars conjunct Venus is considered to be one of the most tempestuous combinations in Vedic astrology. Both these planets have diametrically opposite qualities on all parameters including gana and yoni. Thus this combination sparks extreme behavior in individuals who have Mars conjunct Venus in their horoscope. If Mars and Venus conjoin, the native is fond of betting, gambling or speculation. He may have a large herd of cows. He will have a strong and attractive physique and be attached to other people's wives. Such natives will be proficient in use of metals, minerals and mining elements and will have a scheming nature and be cunning. He will have a respectable position in society and maybe a high ranking dignitary of his clan. He is skilled in mathematics and the sciences but his inherent nature in wicked. He may be under the influence of his spouse.

Table No. 22: Conjunction of Mars and Venus:

House (Bhava)	Results
1st	Native might not be long lived. His conduct is not good. He wastes his wealth on the opposite sex and is attached to people of loose morals.

2nd	Has a harsh speech. Indulges in verbal jousts with people. He may lose his wealth because of affairs with women. Doesn't enjoy good relations with his family.
3rd	Native is combative by nature. He is very popular in the society because of his ability to solve problems. He is courageous and loves taking risks. He has a large female fan following.
4th	The native suffers from constant mental anguish. He is oppressed by various calamities. He has no happiness from children, relations of friends. He will however be rich and have great professional standing in society.
5th	Native runs into trouble because of his passion for entertainment. He doesn't follow the orders of his superiors. He tries his hand at various businesses.
6th	Native doesn't enjoy good relations with his colleagues and may suffer loss of reputation on account of them. He is reckless with his finances which causes him to lose his wealth.
7th	Native has relations with many women. His character is not good. He meets with sorrow and anguish of mind because of the opposite sex.
8th	Native is attracted to foreigners and may marry one. He is religious but might change his religion because of some event. He loves to travel the world and maybe a travel writer. He is generally wealthy.
9th	This is a better placement. Native is intelligent and learned. He has mastery over use of weapons. He is wealthy and leads a life of luxury. He attains fame and occupies a very high rank.
10th	He may be prone to accidents and injuries. His end may be sudden. He has to be careful in matters of finance especially with the opposite sex. Is lustful.
11th	All round gains and prosperity. Lives life on the fast lane. Many friends especially among the opposite sex. He is a master in combat training.
12th	Poor and indolent. Loss on account of opposite sex. Has a voracious appetite for sex. Better to live in foreign lands.

4. Saturn: Mars and Saturn are sworn enemies. None of their qualities match and they generally detest each other's presence. A combination of Mars and Saturn is about as intense as it gets and generally gives a number of negative results. When Mars and Saturn are together, the native commits acts of infamy. He is not truthful and suffers from mental anguish. Native will be contentious but not intelligent. He will however have a flair and be greatly interested in music, dance, drama and acting. He will be irreligious, quarrelsome, and will have a tendency to deceive others. He will be proficient on matters related to the Earth such as petroleum, mining, heavy engineering and machines. He may also be a renowned and talented sportsman. Such a native will also suffer from diseases related to the bile and wind.

Table No. 23: Conjunction of Mars and Saturn:

House (Bhava)	Results
1st	Native may have a medium lifespan. His prosperity is at a low ebb. He does not have cordial relations with his family but is victorious in contest, strife or warfare.
2nd	Native keeps poor health. Money matters result in litigations and disputes which leads to heavy loss in wealth. He suffers from defective speech and is made fun of on account of this. His family is not very supportive of him.
3rd	Native is bold and loves taking big risks although these may land him in trouble. He does well in life after the age of 30. He may be an accomplished sportsman.
4th	Native may be abandoned or boycotted by his relations. He will be sinful in his acts and be devoid of happiness and friends. Inherited lands and properties may result in litigations.
5th	Native suffers on account of his children. He may suffer heavy losses in the stock markets. Investing is not his cup of tea. He also has a number of failed romantic affairs.

6th	Native is courageous and hard-working. He takes on his enemies and defeats them easily. He may borrow heavily to expand his business but ultimately succeeds in enterprise. He attains the position of the head of state.
7th	Native is miserly and oppressed by other people. He is sickly, addicted to vices and leads a humble life. He has no happiness either in respect to his married life or children.
8th	Native is long-lived but his life is spent in litigations and court cases which may also lead to imprisonment. He is argumentative and suffers from bad relations with his family and in-laws. He has a speculative tendency.
9th	Native is irreligious and is a born iconoclast. He may change is religion. He does better in foreign lands. He may be a renowned scientist or engineer whose inventions change humanity for the better.
10th	Native is honored and gains handsomely on account of the king or the government but he may also be punished by them for a major offense. The native is not truthful.
11th	Native will attain a high position in his profession and is popular and famous. He is very wealthy, is the head of a large organization and leads a luxurious life with his family.
12th	Native is poor and devoid of good relations. He suffers from disorders related to the lower abdomen and legs and is prone to injuries. His life is spent in foreign lands although he may turn into an aimless wanderer.

Conjunctions of Mercury:

1. Jupiter: Natives with conjunction of Mercury and Jupiter will be highly skilled and multi-talented individuals with very high levels of intelligence. Both Buddha and Guru are planets of intellect and academics which could result in a native with this combination becoming a renowned academician or educationist or even a world famous philosopher or god man with a mass following. People with this combination have a flair for song, music, dance, drama and acting and may excel in such professions. The native with this conjunction in his horoscope will have a pleasing personality, be of good speech and have many merits. He will be rich, wise and intelligent and lead a comfortable life. At the same time, this combination could also lead to poor eyesight and deafness.

Table No. 24: Conjunction of Mercury and Jupiter:

House (Bhava)	Results
1st	Digbala for both Jupiter and Mercury. Native is endowed with all kinds of comfort, conveyances and articles of luxury. He has a pleasing personality, is courteous, well-behaved and learned. He is respected by the king.
2nd	Native is wealthy and is blessed with a good family. He has a melodious voice and could be a singer, actor or an instrumental musician.
3rd	Native is blessed with a large network of friends. He may be connected to media or journalism and may become a famous author. He has an affable personality, is blessed with great verbal and non-verbal communication skills and has a flair for trading and commerce.
4th	Native is wealthy and gets conjugal happiness. He has properties, conveyances, good friends, relations and leads a happy life. He is clever and is a favourite of the government and the monarch.
5th	Native is blessed with intelligent and attractive children who bring laurels to his family. He may head a business empire and ultimately pass it down to his children. He is lucky in matters of romance.
6th	Native has an attractive appearance and a clever mind. He may get into trouble on matters of money. He may suffer from ear related disorders.
7th	Native has a good, attractive and religious marriage partner. He has great stamina and conquers his enemies. He is a born businessman particularly in the fields of banking and financial services. He has a large number of friends and is wealthy. He rises above the status of his father.

8th	Native might succeed in joint ventures particularly with his spouse and in-laws. Investments may give handsome returns after a period of time. His luck increases after marriage.
9th	Native is a highly educated and deeply religious individual. He may be a poet, preacher or philosopher. He heads a large academic institution of world class repute. He is an inspiration to his students. He lives abroad.
10th	Native may become a king or enjoy the status of one. He is courteous and well-mannered. He commands much respect and his orders are obeyed. He is religious in his outlook and his actions are good.
11th	Native is a highly reputed and famous individual. He is wealthy and always thinks about gains. He tries to help his family, friends and subordinates. He has a good name ins society.
12th	Native is a recluse despite having good communication skills and decent network of friends. He may be a researcher, investigative journalist or a spy.

2. Venus: The conjunction of Mercury and Venus is a fairly common and can be found in the horoscope of many individuals. Mercury signifies intellect, knowledge, communication skills and analytical ability while Venus is the significator for romance, music, dance, drama and entertainment. Thus individuals with this combination in their birth chart will be creative by nature. Such natives will be learned, eloquent and clever in dealing with others. They become leaders among land owners or trade unions. If both Mercury and Venus are strong, the native may occupy a very high position in life, be diplomatic and very wealthy. He is also clever in arts and crafts and develops a highly aesthetic sense. They may have complications arising out of marriage or children.

Table No. 25: Conjunction of Mercury and Venus:

House (Bhava)	Results
1st	Native has a handsome and attractive personality. He will be much respected and a favorite of the king.
2nd	Native comes from a well to do family and multiplies his family wealth. He has cordial relations with everyone but is a sweet talker.
3rd	Native is a born diplomat. His communication skills are second to none and he uses this to resolve complex problems. He excels in the glamor world.
4th	Native has a comely face and figure. He has good relations, children and friends, is blessed with worldly prosperity and occupies a high rank.
5th	Native is blessed with a high quality spouse and obedient children who increase his standing in society. He is wealthy and famous and seeks the company of good people.
6th	Native gets into trouble on money matters but escapes with the help of his maternal uncle. He is often worried and stressed even for the smallest of matters. He is adept at multi-tasking which brings him glory at the workplace.
7th	Native is surrounded by a large number of beautiful women. He is happy, leads a luxurious life and is liked by the king.
8th	Faulty investments may land him in legal trouble. He needs to be very careful with regards to inherited properties.
9th	Native is famous and very wealthy and is blessed with the best spouse and children. He loves travel and adventure and tastes everlasting success in foreign lands.
10th	Native is very diplomatic. He is very capable and executes extraordinarily difficult projects with ease. He occupies a very position in society and becomes very wealthy. He patronizes only good people.
11th	Native becomes exceedingly wealthy. He has a large network friends companions belonging to the opposite sex. He has a flair for using his network to accomplish difficult tasks with relative ease.
12th	Native may have multiple marriages. He may be attached to a number of women of questionable character. Native may succeed in the entertainment industry.

3. Saturn: Natives with Mercury-Saturn conjunction are blessed with a sharp intellect, ability to persevere and highly curious and problem solving mind. They are very hardworking and seldom leave anything to chance. Ancient texts state that such a combination makes the native clever and deceitful. He has a tendency to transgress moral and social laws. Mercury stands for intelligence while Saturn indicates depth. This depth can be used in worldly matters meaning hiding one's own thoughts and thus practicing deception. In highly intelligent people this depth may be used for good cause or a higher purpose. People with such a combination may be scientists or philosophers but they also suffer from neurosis, derangement of brain or lunacy.

Table No. 26: Conjunction of Mercury and Saturn:

House (Bhava)	Results
1st	Native has an uncouth body and lacks good education, wealth and conveyances. His actions are sinful. He is not fortunate and has a short life. He is however blessed with good spouse and children.
2nd	Native has obstruction throughout life in matters of money. He indulges in doublespeak. He does not derive happiness from his family.
3rd	Upachaya house and Saturn's influence may make the native fearless. Native is full of enterprise and is praised for all his good qualities. He has the gift of gab and uses this solve his client's problems. Good for lawyers.
4th	Native's actions are not commendable. He has no good friends or relations. His people forsake him. He does not lead a comfortable life.
5th	Native's creative side often lands him in trouble with the authorities who often see him as nuisance value and a rebel. He may be a gifted and renowned author.

6th	Native speaks sweetly and is clever but runs into debts. He has a tendency to deceive others and is a hypocrite. He is however renowned for his qualities of patience, perseverance and hard work which help him easily defeat his enemies and attain a high position in society. Keeps poor health.
7th	Native has an unclean appearance. He is not truthful nor is his conduct good. He is dull-witted and does not do good to others. He may be in the employment of others.
8th	Native has a long life but is often embroiled in controversies. Corruption charges may be leveled against him on bank related frauds. It is better for him to be an advisor. Could be a psychic.
9th	Native is very wealthy and is blessed with spouse and children of very high quality. If Jupiter is connected, native may be very religious and may teach everyone to follow dharma.
10th	Native vanquishes all his enemies. He has a large army of friends and followers. He is wealthy and has vehicles. He is religious and pays homage to the gods, Brahmins and religious preceptors.
11th	Native reaches a high position in life after the age of 30. He is surrounded by a number of followers and friends. He is wealthy and is blessed with good wife and sons.
12th	Native has a wicked mind and is accused of being a thief. He doesn't maintain cordial relations with his family and prefers to live far away from home. He can use his abilities to help the government catch outlaws and criminals.

Conjunctions of Jupiter:

1. Venus: Jupiter is the guru of the devas or gods while Venus is guru to the asuras or demons. Both are Brahmin planets in the caste system. Being a teacher, they are primary tendency will always to be give something or fortify an individual's life. Conjunction of Jupiter and Venus makes a native with such a combination religious, intelligent, learned and wealthy. He may earn by virtue of his scholarship. He is endowed with meritorious qualities. His marriage partner comes from a noble and high ranking family and he will be blessed with conjugal happiness. He will be chivalrous and a favorite of the monarch or the sovereign.

Table No. 27: Conjunction of Jupiter and Venus:

House (Bhava)	Results
1st	Native will have a forgiving disposition. He goes by the advice given to him by his preceptors and seniors. He attains a high position in life.
2nd	Native comes from a royal lineage and is born with a silver spoon. He is interested in music, fine arts and cinema and could make it his profession. He has a pleasing personality and a lyrical voice.
3rd	Native is soft spoken, docile and well-intentioned. He will gain because of his brothers. He has very good relations with his friends.
4th	Native vanquishes his enemies. He has good friends, relations and vehicles. He pays homage to the gods, Brahmins and religious preceptors.
5th	Native is famous on account of his children. He may have a love marriage. His spouse brings him lots of luck and is blessed with all good qualities. He gains by running a business empire with the support of his sons.
6th	Native may be troubled by some chronic disease. He comes up by sheer dint of his efforts. He may head a large organization.
7th	He has a good marriage and is wealthy. He attains good name and fame in society and leads a comfortable life. He has many properties and conveyances and is blessed with more daughters than sons.
8th	Native inherits a fortune from his family. His in-laws come from a royal lineage. He gets a beautiful spouse and good children. He is long lived and leads a comfortable life. His fortunes rise after marriage.
9th	Native may marry a foreigner or someone who was raised in a foreign land. He is highly educated, spiritual, respects his religious preceptors yet at the same time is highly regarded by people from other religious beliefs. He gets a lot of happiness on account of his spouse and children. He could be a banking professional.
10th	Native is blessed with the best spouse and children. He possesses many luxury items or consumer goods and commands immense respect in society. He is a flexible person. He is wealthy, has a number of servants and occupies a kingly position.

11th	Native may be a wealthy aristocrat. He has many good qualities, a large network of friends. He gets benefits from his elder siblings. He is highly respected in his line of work and in the society at large.
12th	Native gets comforts from association with many women. He succeeds both in his native land as well as in foreign lands. He is interested in arts and crafts.

2. Saturn: Jupiter is the planet that indicates wisdom, luck and optimism while Saturn indicates hard work, struggles, adversity and perseverance. Although their qualities are completely different to one another, Jupiter and Saturn are not enemies and can give good rewards in conjunction if the placement doesn't have external malefic influences. Classic texts on astrology state that when Jupiter and Saturn are together, the native is chivalrous and wealthy. He may be the mayor of a town or the president of a multinational organization or the head of state of an influential country. He attains good name and fame. He may excel as a craftsman, barber or as a manufacturer of utensils or may even deal in grain or food products. Such an individual is generally quite generous. Results are generally mixed when Jupiter and Saturn combine as at the end of the day Jupiter stands for happiness while Saturn signifies sorrows.

Table No. 28: Conjunction of Jupiter and Saturn:

House (Bhava)	Results
1st	Native is indolent and cruel. He is learned and wealthy, but will have only a fraction of happiness. He is wicked. Results are better in the rashis of Jupiter (Dhanu and Meena).
2nd	Native is learned and wealthy and is respected by his peers. He invites the wrath of the authorities for his accumulation of wealth and may face court cases on account of this. He is lethargic by nature.

3rd	Native is chivalrous, courageous and a born leader among men. He has good relations with his brother and has a flair for doing business for short term gains.
4th	Native will have good friends and relations. He will be on affectionate terms with others. He will have good health and become a minister. He will be victorious in a contest, strife or warfare.
5th	Native may face delays in producing children but they bring him great benefits after their birth. Native prefers to work on his own or run a business empire rather than being a salaried professional.
6th	Native is hardworking but is cruel towards his subordinates. He makes many enemies but defeats them ultimately. He suffers from ailments in the lower part of his body.
7th	Native will be chivalrous but addicted to some kind of vice. He will be wicked and unattractive. He will be dull-witted and avaricious of his father's wealth. He will lose his wealth on account of enmity with a woman or with woman generally.
8th	May live past the age of 90. Benefits financially after marriage particularly after the age of 30. He may be an astrologer, palmist, psychic or even a renowned god man.
9th	Native benefits on account of his father and inherits properties from him. But this may also cause some issues. He is well-mannered and well-intentioned, is a favorite of the king and maintains a high position in society.
10th	Native owns many cattle and conveyances. He has only a few sons. He is a favorite of the king and occupies a high position.
11th	Native has many properties and conveyances. He is known to work hard to achieve all his goals. He heads a large multinational organization and may be recognized and remembered well after his lifetime for his inventions.
12th	Native is wicked, unfriendly and cruel. He may be addicted to gambling, drugs and alcohol. He is better off staying away from his home to avoid disputes and quarrels.

Conjunctions of Venus:

1. Saturn: Venus, the planet of money, romance, merriment and entertainment, and Saturn, the planet of discipline, hard work, and determination are known to be the best of friends. Together they can make the native one of the wealthiest on the face of the Earth. Venus conjunct Saturn makes the native a master in music, dance, instrumental music, drawing, painting and calligraphy. His wealth multiplies because of his association with the opposite sex. Ancient texts state that such a native will be an athlete and own cattle. He loves traveling the world. He may be a renowned surgeon or a skilled craftsman or even be involved in timber work or artisanship.

Table No. 29: Conjunction of Venus and Saturn:

House (Bhava)	Results
1st	Native has an amiable personality and many sexual liaisons. He is rich and leads a comfortable life. He has a number of servants but suffers sorrows.
2nd	After some initial obstruction, native gets the riches and leads a luxurious life. He is not honest and may not respected by the society despite of his high standing.
3rd	Native is renowned for his valor, courage and stamina. He exceeds in executing difficult tasks and gets the support of the opposite sex in all his ventures.
4th	Native gains money from his friends and is respected by his relations. He also receives honours and riches from the government.
5th	Native enjoys sexual liaisons with many women and is known for his many romances. He is wealthy, chivalrous and exhibits leadership traits. He is connected to the entertainment industry.
6th	Native is hard working, clever and indulges in double speak. He climbs the corporate ladder with the help of his superiors.
7th	Native will be under the control of his spouse, is very wealthy and occupies a high rank under the king. He enjoys sexual pleasures and surrounds himself with damsels. He earns a good reputation.

8th	Native loves the company and the pleasures associated with the opposite sex. He may start a build a successful business with his spouse. He prefers investing in unconventional art forms.
9th	Native is under the control of his spouse who may be a foreigner but has all good qualities. He is wealthy and of good repute. He loves anything artistic and may make a career out of music or dance.
10th	Native may become a minister or king. He is an aristocrat who performs noble deeds, becomes famous and is free from all mental perplexities.
11th	Native is among the wealthiest in the planet. He has high levels of physical and mental stamina and prefers to be in the company of the opposite sex.
12th	Native may be involved in some sex scandal which may cost him his job. He succeeds in foreign lands and earns a good reputation there.

Chapter 5

Aspects in Vedic Astrology

In the chapter on planetary conjunctions, we studied the impact of having two planets placed in the same house. In this chapter, we are going to take a closer look at the effect that will be produced when a planet aspects another planet.

The English word 'aspect' is known by the Sanskrit term 'drishti' which indicates what happens when an entity looks at or glances at another entity. As human beings, we have often heard about the positive or negative luck that comes our way based on the good or bad drishti of a supernatural force. It is the same with planets. When one planet aspects another, it alters the good or bad effects that the planet that is aspected can produce (If planet 'A' aspects planet 'B', then 'A' is the aspector and 'B' is the aspected planet).

In this chapter, we will limit our discussions on planetary aspects to the Sun, Moon, Mars, Mercury, Jupiter, Venus and Saturn. We will exclude the shadow planets, Rahu and Ketu when talking about aspects.

Planetary aspects vary in Vedic astrology based on the planets involved in the aspect, the signs or rashis which the two planets 'A' and 'B' own or are situated in and of course the houses where they are placed.

Also, like in the case of drishti, aspects need not necessarily be entirely good or bad. They can give mixed results. Intuitively, this would indicate to me that an aspector can give mixed results to the aspected planet.

Finally, when we talk about drishtis, we say that they have varying degrees of intensity indicating that the drishtis can be partial and need not be full. Applying the same principle in Vedic astrology, we see that a planet 'A' aspects another planet 'B' to varying degrees of intensities. Aspects can be anywhere between 0 to 100% based on the rashis and houses that the two planets concerned are placed in.

Again, for the sake of simplicity, we are going to assume a full aspect or 100% aspect in this book when we look at various combinations of planetary aspects.

A planet 'A' is known to fully aspect (100% aspect) or cast its drishti on another planet 'B' when the 2 planets are exactly opposite to each other in a rashi chart or a divisional chart, meaning they are in the 7th rashi or 7th house from each other. The 7th house aspect is a 2-way relationship as 'B' will also aspect 'A'.

For example, the planet of Sun if placed in Aries or Mesha rashi will aspect any planet 'B' placed in Libra or Tula rashi. Planet B in turn will aspect Sun.

According to classical texts in astrology:-

Six planets Sun, Moon, Mercury, Venus, Rahu and Ketu fully aspect (100% aspect) the 7th rashi from where they are placed in a horoscope.

Mars in addition to fully aspecting the 7th rashi also aspects the 4th and 8th rashis clockwise from where it is placed in the birth chart.

Jupiter in addition to fully aspecting the 7th rashi also aspects the 5th and 9th rashis clockwise from where it is placed in the birth chart.

Saturn in addition to fully aspecting the 7th rashi also aspects the 3rd and 10th rashis clockwise from where it is placed in the birth chart.

Revisiting Rashis:

The 12 rashis from Aries (Mesha) to Pisces (Meena) could be classified based on the following parameters:-

1. Modality:

(a) **Initiator Signs:** They are born leaders who initiate projects and act according to their aims and goals. Mesha, Kataka, Tula and Makara are the four initiator signs.

(b) **Fixed Signs:** Status quoists who believe in continuity and a desire to build on what is already established. They love to consolidate and are born organizers. Vrishaba, Simha, Vrischika and Kumbha are the four fixed signs.

(c) **Mutable Signs:** They seek change, renewal and realignment. They are known to be flexible and adjust themselves according to the situation. Mithuna, Kanya, Dhanu and Meena are the mutable signs.

2. Elements:

(a) **Fire Signs:** People born under a fire sign are spontaneous and act on impulse and intuition and apply their energies wholeheartedly. Their emotional response is quick and they have a lively imagination. Mesha, Simha and Dhanu are the three fire signs.

(b) **Earth Signs:** Earth is a security conscious element and the most practical among the four. Earthy people react quietly and slowly. They apply themselves with endurance. Emotionally they are deeply rooted and slow to change. Vrishaba, Kanya and Makara are the earth signs.

(c) **Air Signs:** Air is the most intellectual and innovative element. It is unconcerned with the material side of life and is driven by a desire to communicate and share thought. Airy people are quick and animated. They apply their energies in very diverse ways and are full of novel ideas and new possibilities. Mithuna, Tula and Kumbha are the three air signs.

(d) **Water Signs:** Water is the most subtle and sensitive of elements. This is the least outwardly aware of the elements and the most irrational. People with a strongly emphasized water element are very sensitive as water is connected with feeling, cycles and fluctuations. Their imaginative and emotional lives are deep and rich. The three water signs are Kataka, Vrischika and Meena.

Classic astrology classifies the 12 rashis or zodiacs on the basis of both their element and modality. So how does one go about finding specific differences between any 2 rashis? Kumbha rashi or Aquarius is a fixed air sign and thus will exhibit qualities of its modality such as stubbornness/inflexibility in its quest to maintain status quo. Additionally, per its elemental classification of air it exhibits innovation and intellect. Aquarians thus are driven by novelty yet they could desire to maintain status quo and consolidate and execute on existing norms. Contrast this with another air sign Tula rashi or Libra which will exhibit similar novelty but will have an uninhibited desire to take leadership and craft a strategy on such ideas.

Table No. 30: Element and Modality of Rashis (Planet in bracket indicates planet owning the sign):

	Fire	Earth	Air	Water
Cardinal	Mesha (Mars)	Makara (Saturn)	Tula (Venus)	Kataka (Moon)
Fixed	Simha (Sun)	Vrishaba (Venus)	Kumbha (Saturn)	Vrischika (Mars)
Mutable	Dhanu (Jupiter)	Kanya (Mercury)	Mithuna (Mercury)	Meena (Jupiter)

With the above information of the 12 rashis, let us now jump into planetary aspects of the 7 planets based on its placement and aspect on specific rashis in Vedic astrology.

Aspects of Sun:

Sun is a sattvik / pure planet or a planet of the devas in the pantheon of the navagrahas. It is considered a malefic planet as it burns anyone that goes near it. Sun is the centre of our universe and thus it signifies power, prestige and fame. Thus, it tries to impart these qualities or it might induce this behaviour on the planets it is aspecting. For example, Sun placed in Aries is exalted and it is aspecting Moon in Libra it may make the individual a fiery person who wants to take a leadership role in professions connected to Moon such as the glamour world. Of course we also have to consider other points such as the house number, lagna, ownership of the rashis and influence of other planets.

As the planets or Mercury and Venus can at most be placed at a distance of 27° and 48° respectively from the Sun, both these planets can never be aspected by the Sun. Mercury is at most placed one house away from the Sun, while Venus is at most placed 2 houses away from the Sun.

Table No. 31: Aspects of Sun on various planets placed in:

	Moon	Mars	Jupiter	Saturn
Mesha / Vrischika	Native can be haughty in disposition and persevering. He is learned, rich and loves traveling. He may not be popular especially when Moon is in Vrischika but has a benevolent attitude towards people.	Wealthy, blessed with wife and sons. Occupies position of authority where he may punish others. Renowned and generous.	Religious, learned, honest and wealthy. Son becomes famous.	Native is hard working and prospers after the age of 30. He may succeed in agriculture related activities.
Vrishaba / Tula	Industrious, wealthy (especially when Moon in Vrishaba), loves luxuries and centerstage, connected to agriculture. Has to work very hard to gain wealth when Moon in Tula.	Fiery temperament. Problems in married life. Many adversaries. Visits mountains and forests.	Owns land, property and cattle. Heftily built. Loves traveling. Wise, learned and rises to the top.	Delicately built frame. Wealth after much obstruction. Articulate and learned.
Mithuna / Kanya	Could be religious and learned. Wise in communication. May be a finance professional. Connected to government. Difficulties in marriage. Wealth accumulation takes time.	Courageous. High levels of stamina. Loves travelling. Learned and wealthy.	Occupies a high position. Could be a head of a nation, city or village. Wealthy and blessed with wife and children.	Not very happy in life. Religious and educated. Persevering by nature. Obstruction in money matters.

Kataka	Moon's sign. Engages in government service but devoid of wealth. He may be an administrator or a military man. Takes stress.	Assertive and perseverant. May be a judge.	Jupiter exalted. Born leader of men. Famous. Has to put lot of effort to become wealthy. Some problems in family life.	Separation from family early on in life is possible. Poor appetite. Problems with money. Family life not good.
Simha	Sun's sign. Conflicts with government and higher authorities. Heroic and occupies exalted position.	Outdoor person. Lot of friends. Fiery by nature. Patronizes people who support him.	Friendly and genteel. Rises to a kingly position. Famous. Wealthy and gets all luxuries of life.	Sun and Saturn in sign exchange. Native is poor, devoid of wealth, dependent on others. He has a sickly body, is unhappy and is prone to excesses in life.
Dhanu / Meena	Native is wealthy and leads a luxurious life. Lucky in marriage and sex. Has luxury goods and vehicles.	Attractive. Wants to lead a quiet life in the village. Respected but unfriendly by nature.	Major obstructions in wealth accumulation. Deserted by relatives. Has mental problems. Antagonistic in nature to authorities.	Native lives vicariously. Has relations with many women of questionable character. He may benefit from them.
Makara / Kumbha	Proficient and skilled in military matters and or as a craftsman. Slovenly appearance. Works very hard. Gains from agriculture and land. May not be rich.	Leadership material. Courageous, wealthy. Has wife and sons. Aggressive by nature.	Wealthy, prosperous and occupies a high position in society. Has a helping nature. Blessed with good friends and family. Intelligent and heroic by nature.	Lots of physical hardships. Dependent on others. Travels and wanders a lot. Keeps poor health. Appearance is not good. Conjugal issues.

Example 16:

Venus	Sun	Mercury	Ketu
			Asc Moon Jupiter
Mars			
Rahu		Saturn (R)	

This birth chart is that of a legendary king and very famous Hindu god of India. Five planets, namely, Jupiter, Saturn, Mars, Venus and Sun are all exalted. Moon is in its own house. Aspect of Sun on Saturn meant the native had to undergo all types of trials and tribulations to ascend the throne of his empire. He was an exceptionally skilled individual who was articulate and very learned.

Aspects of Moon:

Moon is the most soft and feeble planet among the navagrahas. Like the Sun, it is a planet of the gods but is considered a benefic. If placed well in a natal chart, it will always try and give wisdom, a strong mind and a good heart as well as bless the native with a royal and luxurious life and grant him gains connected to the glamour world. If Moon is afflicted, it can give the native mental health issues, high levels of stress leading to decay and trouble with women. It may also take the native down an immoral path. These qualities are then imparted on the planets it aspects. For example, Moon aspecting Jupiter in Sagittarius blesses the native with wealth and favours from the opposite sex. A waxing Moon (Shukla paksha) will generally provide better results when compared to a waning Moon (Krishna paksha).

A widely acknowledged aspect in astrology is Moon's mutual aspect with Jupiter that gives rise to the Gaja Kesari yoga. This yoga makes the native a highly renowned individual whose inventions and thoughts benefit mankind in such a manner that he is fondly recalled by the society much after his lifetime. Such people are also known to lead highly contended lives. They are wealthy and prosperous.

Table No. 32: Aspects of Moon on various planets placed in:

Part A:

	Sun	Mars	Mercury	Jupiter
Mesha / Vrischika	Soft and attractive body. Attachment to damsels. Charitable by nature.	Unhappy on account of mother. Envious but fond of girls. Has no friends. Boils on body.	Attractive to opposite sex. Conduct is not good. Appears shabby and serves others.	Native is an expert in history, drama and poetry. He is intelligent, learned and occupies a high position. He possesses jewels and favours from the opposite sex.
Vrishaba / Tula	Soft spoken. Monetary gains through water related articles. Very lucky with young women.	Connections with a number of women. Not friendly with mother. Lacks courage and boldness.	Wealthy and reliable. Religious, renowned and occupies an exalted position. Good health and good family life.	Soft-spoken. Receives the affection of mothers. Very popular with women. Enjoys life.

Mithuna / Kanya	Trouble in life on account of enemies. Wanderer. Suffers in faraway lands.	Attractive and courteous. May work under a powerful monarch.	Sweet but talkative. Successful in life. Bookish but quarrelsome.	Native is handsome and rich. He leads a happy life. He gets wife and sons. His mother is fond of him. He is mild-mannered and very gentle.
Kataka	Monetary gains through water related articles. Occupies an exalted position. Unfriendly by nature.	Occupies administrative position. Bold, aggressive and hard-working.	Energy wasted on account of women. Leads an unhappy and sickly life because of them.	Native is wealthy and has a very attractive personality. He occupies a high position in life and possess all types of luxury items. His mother is renowned.
Simha	Favourite of the sovereign or king. Intelligent and gets good wife.	Intelligent and wealthy. Gains through women. Separation from mother.	Handsome. Wealthy. Loves women and all finer aspects of life like, arts, dance and poetry.	Native has high morals and great level of self-control. He has an attractive personality. He becomes wealthy because of his wife. He is courteous and friendly.

Dhanu / Meena	Good body. Peaceful mind. Happy and prosperous in life. Intelligent and renowned.	Intelligent and well-educated. Quarrelsome and restless. Opposes authority.	Good writer. Tender body. Wealthy and luxurious. His conduct is praised.	Native is wealthy and owns many luxury items. He is attractive to women and is held in high esteem by the society.
Makara / Kumbha	Deceptive. Can hide his thoughts. Loses wealth and happiness on account of women.	Problems with mother. Fickle but generous. Wealth accumulation takes time. Possesses land and jewellery.	Wealthy and prosperous. Monetary gains through water related goods. Not bold. Gains also through spirits and alcohol.	Native possesses good conduct. He is devoted to his parents. He comes from a very good family, is religious and down to earth.

Part B:

	Venus	Saturn
Mesha / Vrischika	May be connected to women of low class. Wife may come from such backgrounds. Active by nature but has changeable disposition.	Active but fickle minded. Attached to older and unattractive women. Lacks wealth and happiness.
Vrishaba / Tula	Comes from a high status family. Problems with sons. Wealthy and luxurious life. Attractive personality and agreeable disposition.	Has lady luck. Becomes wealthy because of them. Blessed with large family and is appreciated for his work by the government and rewarded by them.

Mithuna / Kanya	Attractive appearance and tender body with dark hair and black eyes. Enjoys comforts of the bed and leads a comfortable life.	Works for ladies. Gets lucky and wealthy because of them. Occupies a dignified position. He has a smooth and lustrous body.
Kataka	Native has stepmother. His first child is daughter then several sons are born. He is attractive, soft and leads a happy life.	Sign exchange between Moon and Saturn. Not good for mother. Doesn't have good relations with siblings. Wealthy in life.
Simha	Wealthy but suffers on account of his wife or other women on account of frustrations caused by them. Fickle minded.	Possesses jewellery and lots of money. Famous and enjoys the company of women. Rewarded by the government.
Dhanu / Meena	Native enjoys all luxuries of life including women, food and drink. High levels of stamina. Occupies a chief position under the monarch.	Wealthy and blessed with wife and sons. Courteous and friendly. Relationship with mother may not be good. May separate from her.
Makara / Kumbha	Native is bold and courageous and high levels of stamina and moral fibre. He has a good body and attractive personality.	Fickle-minded, dishonest and sinful in conduct. Wealth accumulation after lots of efforts. Problems with mother here.

Example 17:

Mercury	Sun		Rahu
Venus			Moon
Asc Mars Jupiter			
Ketu	Saturn (R)		

Above is the birth chart of a very famous monarch of the planet. This horoscope is blessed with a number of raja yogas with one among them being the Gaja Kesari yoga on account of the mutual aspect between Moon and Jupiter. As mentioned in Table No. 32, this aspect takes place with Jupiter in Makara rashi and Moon in Kataka rashi (its own sign). Native comes from a royal family and is known to be courteous, religious is known to have been devoted to her parents. As per the traditions of her dynasty, she ascended the throne at the young age of 26 after the demise of her father. She is known to have a level-headed mind and has tried to impart the same set of ideals in her family. She is wealthy and has been long lived. The mahadasha of Venus which is a yogakaraka (Owner of the 5th and 10th house) in this birth chart resulted in her becoming the Queen of her country.

Aspects of Mars:

Mars is also a planet of the devas. It is the planet of action, fire and relentless energy that loves talking leadership roles. It is known as the military commander among the nine planets. This is the type of action it will try and impart on the planets it aspects. It makes the native injury prone and rash.

Remember, in addition to the 7th house aspect, Mars also fully aspects the 4th and 8th house from where it sits. Thus, when Mars aspects another planet one must take into account the houses Mars owns, the house that it is placed in along with its dignity in the shadbala table and apply the same principle on the planet it aspects.

For example, when Mars aspects the Sun in its signs of Mesha and Vrischika which are positive for the Sun also, Mars will make the native courageous and not give up without a fight. He will be heroic and will possess a lot of strength.

Table No. 33: Aspects of Mars on various planets placed in:

Part A:

	Sun	Moon	Mercury	Jupiter
Mesha / Vrischika	Courageous and pugnacious. Reddish complexion. Heroic. High levels of stamina.	Occupies a high position in society. May suffer from eye or dental troubles. Wealthy. Perseverant and courageous in all situations.	Quarrelsome and dishonest. Learned, courageous and favourite of the authorities. Wealthy.	Courteous and diplomatic. Does not have a happy marriage. Works for the king. Courageous and aggressive.
Vrishaba / Tula	Loves a battle. Heroic. Wealth and fame after lots of hard work. Restless.	Goes after other women. He is adored by young women. Separation from mother. Intelligent and short tempered.	Suffers chronic diseases. Difficulties on account of sovereign and the monarch. Unhappy in life.	Clever, courageous and wealthy. Serves the king. Loved by the opposite sex.
Mithuna / Kanya	Quarrelsome. Suffers humiliation and is distressed. Shy and diffident.	Learned, courageous, wealthy, happy and good-looking. Problems with mother. Skilled in arts and crafts.	Intelligent. Serves the king. Dresses shabbily but is still very popular. Body may have scars or wounds.	Rich and indulgent. Popular and commands respect. Infirmity in limbs.
Kataka	Suffers from inflammatory diseases. Distressed and a back-biter. Poor relations with family.	Courageous, clever, and wealthy. May have questionable health. Problems with mother.	Not very learned but talkative. Sweet-talker and dishonest. Scheming and thievish instincts.	Marries early or has a young wife. Intelligent and wealthy. Heroic in nature.

Simha	Courageous. Holds high position. Accomplishes difficult tasks through hard work. Attached to others' wives.	Maybe a policeman or a military officer. Renowned and successful. Blessed with wealth, luxuries, wife and sons.	Suffers from scars and wounds. Morals and ethics are questionable and he suffers distress. Unhappy. Not clever but attractive.	Cruel and aggressive. Truthful and devoted to seniors and gurus. Leads a clean and healthy life.
Dhanu / Meena	Fiery temper. Wins battles. Happy and wealthy. Articulate.	Head of a military institution. Good-looking, wealthy and renowned. Helpful but may commit sins as a result maybe devoid of happiness.	Writer. Could be head of a large multi-national organization or head of state.	Injury prone. He is cruel and has a propensity to hurt others.
Makara / Kumbha	Suffers on account of enemies. Diseased. Quarrels with others. Restless nature.	Attractive, truthful, wealthy, luxurious, fiery and generous. In Kumbha obstruction in wealth accumulation. Salaried professional.	Bashful, lazy, gentle but eloquent in speech. Leads a comfortable life.	Connected to the army. Heroic by nature. Proud and assertive. Of good conduct and respected in society.

Part B:

	Venus	Saturn
Mesha / Vrischika	Works as a sub-ordinate. Devoid of wealth, happiness and respect. His actions are not respectable.	Native is intent on killing. Cruel and thievish instincts. Fond of women, wine and meat. Famous.

Vrishaba / Tula	Wife is ill-tempered. Neglects wife for other women.	Wealthy and surrounded by people. Talkative and an expert in warfare but generally avoids it.
Mithuna / Kanya	Comely appearance but is amorous. Squanders his wealth for the sake of young women.	Excels as a wrestler. Pugnacious and combative. Emotions can get the better of him.
Kataka	Rich and proficient. Attractive personality. Relations prosper because of him but he suffers distress on account of women.	Wealthy. May have some disorder in the limbs. Trouble with government.
Simha	Occupies a high position under a king. Charming personality. Favourite of young ladies. Gains riches because of them. Liaisons with many girls.	Wanderer or frequent traveller but it may not pay dividends. Lives in forests or mountains or other remote locations. Thievish tendencies. Unhappy with wife and children.
Dhanu / Meena	Wealthy but envied by women. Unhappy but has lots of vehicles and land.	Wind related disorders. Actions are mean and sinful. Envious of others.
Makara / Kumbha	Sickly. Wife dies prematurely and he is distressed. Works hard and is happy in later part of life.	Heroic and aggressive. Famous and celebrated. Occupies an eminent position. Hard-working, courageous and sharp.

Example 18:

	Moon	Saturn (R)	
Ketu			Jupiter (R)
			Rahu
	Asc Sun Venus (C)	Mercury (C) Mars (C)	

Above is the birth chart of a famous politician of the United States of America who served as the country's vice president. Mars aspects Moon as well as Saturn which makes him wealthy and blesses him with high positions in his chosen profession and high levels of respect in society. At the same time, the aspect on Moon indicates he has suffered trauma in his personal life and keeps poor health in general. Mars's aspect on functional malefic Saturn in particular indicates loss from marriage. Native's first marriage ended when his wife died in an accident.

Aspects of Mercury:

Mercury is a unique planet among the navagrahas. It is known for its speed, agility and execution capabilities. It is known as the prince among the planets and moves in tandem with the Sun and is the closest to the king among the planets. It acts as a benefic when it is in the company of the benefics and turns into a malefic when in association with malefics. As it is closely placed to the Sun as well as Venus in the rashi chart, it can never aspect these two planets fully (100% aspect).

Mercury is a very mutable planet and changes its behaviour based on the signs it owns, its placement in various houses and also the type of aspect it receives from the planet it in turn aspects. Remember, a 100% aspect of Mercury on another planet is a 7th house aspect which means that the planet it aspects will in turn aspect Mercury.

Mercury's mutual aspect with Jupiter will always enhance outcomes associated with education, learning, speech, with and humour, creative abilities, wisdom and lateral thinking abilities.

Table No. 34: Aspects of Mercury on various planets placed in:

	Moon	Mars	Jupiter	Saturn
Mesha / Vrischika	Learned and erudite. Speaks well (For Moon in Vrischika, speech not very clear). Artistic. Maybe a poet or singer. Earns fame and adulation.	Native gets wealthy through others. Loves sex. Liaison with many women. Untruthful.	Dishonest. He is a cheat and finds flaws in others. Hypocrite. Courteous and helps those who are nice to him.	Dishonest, irreligious, gluttonous and thievish disposition. Lacks happiness and luxuries.
Vrishaba / Tula	Intelligent, cheerful, good speech. Wealthy, learned and famous.	Talkative. Quarrels a lot. He is learned and has a soft body. Obstruction in wealth accumulation.	Intelligent, sweet and clever. Has pleasing personality, courteous, well-bred and good- tempered. Materialistic.	Jocular and jovial. Works for women. Of low disposition.
Mithuna / Kanya	Clever, efficient, perseverant and money making. Maybe a poet or astrologer.	Mathematical, poetic, writer and calligrapher. Ability to undergo stress, strain and hardship. Speaks sweetly but is not truthful.	Astrologer, author, has wives and sons. Expressive and can present his case in many ways.	Well-versed in fine arts, music and dance. Wealthy, clever in battle. Efficient in arts and crafts.
Kataka	Intelligent, diplomatic and occupies a high position. He is rich and has wife and sons.	Native is uncouth, unclean and of bad conduct. Limited family but has problems on account of them.	Wealthy, has many friends and relations. Quarrelsome. Counsellor or adviser.	Cruel, talkative, defeats his enemies. Actions are good but is a hypocrite.

Simha	Native has feminine traits, attractive to women and under their influence. Has luxuries, is wealthy and happy.	Native is good in arts, crafts and poetry. He is greedy, clever and capable.	Learned, artistic, virtuous. Occupies a high position like a minister. Sweet speech.	Indolent, uncouth in appearance and humble. Lacks wealth and works for women.
Dhanu / Meena	Native has a number of servants, occupies an eminent position, is happy and is surrounded by women. Skilled and learned in arts and crafts.	Strong memory power and clever. Learned, efficient and strong in arts and crafts.	Wealthy, happy and many sons. Popular and loved by all. Occupies a high position like a minister.	Scholarly. Lives life like a king. Wealthy and happy. Gentle nature and respected in society.
Makara / Kumbha	Fickle, lacks intelligence and lives abroad. Surrounded by women, loves singing and enjoys sex.	Loves traveling but lacks stamina. Devoid of wealth. Irreligious and a hypocrite.	Wealthy, landed and propertied with many vehicles. Amorous. Has many friends and is renowned.	Capable of putting up with physical hardships. Well-groomed, endowed with knowledge and praised for his actions. Not wealthy.

Example 19:

	Moon	Jupiter (R)	Asc Rahu
Saturn (R)			Mars
			Venus
Ketu		Sun Mercury (C)	

The birth chart shown here is that of a lady politician of the United States who served as her state's attorney general before becoming a senator of her state. She has had a meteoric rise in her professional career before becoming the vice-presidential candidate of her country at the time of writing this book. Mercury's aspect on Moon has given her a strong and sharp mind and ability to talk her way out of situations. She is known for her eloquent speech and has earned much acclaim in her legal and political careers.

Aspects of Jupiter:

Jupiter is the best benefic. It is a planet of the devas. It acts as a guide, teacher, and philosopher and tries to impart knowledge and wisdom as well as spread joy and optimism. Its job is to always try and bring out the best in everyone and hone their abilities and hidden talents. Not surprisingly, when Jupiter aspects any planet, it will always try and bring out these traits in them. For example, Jupiter's aspect on Saturn is a classic case of two powerful planets with polar opposite qualities that are surprisingly neutral in their attitude towards each other, trying to give their own results with Jupiter trying to bring calmness, optimism to match Saturn's qualities of hard-work, perseverance, tolerance and discipline. This combination if combined in the right houses and rashis could produce extraordinary results which may take the native to the zenith of his profession.

Jupiter, in addition to the 7th house aspect, also fully aspects (100% aspect) the 5th and 9th house from where it sits. Thus, when Jupiter aspects another planet one must take into account the houses Jupiter owns, the house that it is placed in along with its dignity in the shadbala table and apply the same principle on the planet it aspects. Jupiter, like Mars, may aspect another planet without it being aspected by that very same planet.

Table No. 35: Aspects of Jupiter on various planets placed in:

Part A:

	Sun	Moon	Mars	Mercury
Mesha / Vrischika	Wealthy and generous. Occupies a high position under the king. Genteel breed.	Wealthy. Has a number of servants. Military commander or king's minster. Good looking. Envied.	Handsome, sweet, intelligent. Wealthy. Has many luxuries. Good parents and wife.	Smooth body. Lots of hair on head. Wealthy and leads a comfortable life. Occupies a high position in life.
Vrishaba / Tula	Has friends and enemies both. Rises to a very high level in profession. Loves to work. Beautiful and attractive eyes.	Happy, healthy, wealthy, religious, capable and blessed with good parents, wife and children. Famous. Clever in dealing with jewellery and artefacts.	Loves music, singing and dancing. Good relations. Clean habits. Prosperous.	Learned and intelligent. Accepts good advice. Occupies a prominent position. Famous.
Mithuna / Kanya	All-rounder. Very knowledgeable. Lives overseas. May be an ambassador. Fiery by nature. Loves excesses.	Truthful. Attractive appearance. All-rounder with wide variety of skill sets. Eloquent. Famous and respected. Good relations with people. Works for government.	Ambassador in a foreign country. Diplomat or administrative officer. Highly capable and comes into limelight for his work.	Handsome, generous, highly skilled, good speech. Long-lived, happy has a large and happy family and rises in profession.

Kataka	Military commander or a king. Famous. Expert in fine arts.	Royal bearing. Kingly appearance and position. Happy, courageous, diplomatic, friendly. Gets good wife and sons.	Learned, famous and praised for his work by government. Lacks luxuries.	Intelligent. Good memory. Highly learned. Prosperous, loved by all, and a favourite of the authority.
Simha	Intelligent. Loner. Good stamina. Builds temples and monuments.	Scion of a royal or famous family. Learned and endowed with many good qualities. Occupies a kingly position.	Intelligent, clear mind. Could be a professor, staff of a king or heads an army.	Soft and elegant body. Intelligent and learned. Good speech. Has lands, properties, servants and vehicles.
Dhanu / Meena	Wealthy. Learned. Lives life king sized. Maybe a king himself.	Wealthy, religious, pleasing personality, favourite of damsels, occupies a big position. Happy.	Wealthy. Physically strong. Problems in marriage.	Writer, treasurer, banker, scientist. Highly skilled, intelligent, good-looking and blessed with a good family.
Makara / Kumbha	Intelligent. Famous. Helpful. Hardworking and praised by all.	Surrounded by beautiful damsels. Owns villages, lands and orchards. Happy, wealthy, respected and occupies a kingly position. Happy family life.	Good relations with people. Endowed with kingly qualities. Works diligently. Long-lived and not handsome.	Wealthy. Leads a comfortable life. Famous. Receives homage from his native place.

Part B:

	Venus	Saturn
Mesha / Vrischika	Native has attractive eyes and a good, large body. He is blessed with a good and generous wife and several sons.	Native is endowed with wealth and happiness. He becomes minister to the king and occupies a high position in the government.
Vrishaba / Tula	Fortunate with regards to wife, sons, properties and vehicles. Engages in good work.	Native works for others and tries to solve their problems. He is generous and caring. He partakes in others joys and sorrows.
Mithuna / Kanya	Happy. Humility in abundance. Learned and scholarly. Can be a professor. Good at copying.	Liked by the gentry. Endowed with many fine qualities. Trusted in royal circles. Wealthy.
Kataka	Blessed with sons, relations, friends and servants. Favourite of the king. Wealthy and commands many vehicles and luxuries.	Owns many fields and houses. Blessed with wife, sons, friends, and jewellery.
Simha	Many love affairs and marriages. Wealthy and commands vehicles and servants. Occupies the position of a minister.	Person of great repute in his village or town. Blessed with sons. Courteous and sweet-tempered. Relied upon by people.
Dhanu / Meena	Leads a happy life. Blessed with good wife and sons. Wealthy and owns many properties and vehicles.	He overcomes any impediments in life with ease. He is a commander of army or king. Prominent person of the planet.
Makara / Kumbha	Gets a good wife. Loves music, singing and dancing. Soft and elegant body. Fond of fine apparel, flowers and scents.	Native has many admirable qualities. He is long-lived and healthy. He works for the sovereign and attains a high position.

Example 20:

		Rahu	Jupiter (R)
Saturn (R)			
Moon			Asc
Venus	Mercury Ketu Mars	Sun	

The above birth chart is that of a highly renowned and famous film personality of India. He entered the entertainment industry towards the end of his Rahu mahadasha and rose to the zenith of his profession during the 16 years of his Jupiter mahadasha. Jupiter's aspect on Sun, Venus and Saturn has blessed with an attractive personality, name and fame in his profession, a good wife and good children and loads of wealth. Retrograde Jupiter's aspect on retrograde Saturn in particular has made him extremely hardworking by nature. He is likely to be long-lived and continue to earn plaudits in life.

Aspects of Venus:

Venus is the planet of beauty, love, pleasures of life, entertainment and romance. Like Jupiter, it is a benefic but is an asura graha and guru to the danavs. Also, like Jupiter, it is a planet of wealth and luxuries but unlike Jupiter, it craves for materialistic and creature comforts. Venus will always try and transmit its inherent qualities onto the planet that it aspects. This may give the native all the wealth he desires but at the same time get him embroiled in controversies related to women. For example, Venus aspecting Mars may result in the native having liaisons with a number of women in life but the same time, such an individual may have high levels of physical energy which may make him a military commander. Again, one needs to look into the ascendant, ownership and placement of Venus in the birth chart and the planet(s) that it aspects before arriving at a conclusion.

Venus fully aspects (100% aspect) the 7th house from where it sits.

Also, as mentioned in the sections on the aspects of Sun and Mercury, Venus can never fully aspect Sun and Mercury as it moves through the zodiac in tandem with these two planets. At most, Venus can be 48° away from the Sun and 65° away from Mercury in a rashi chart.

Table No. 36: Aspects of Venus on various planets placed in:

	Moon	Mars	Jupiter	Saturn
Mesha / Vrischika	Good-looking. Blessed with best wife and sons. Intelligent. Wealthy. Owns properties and vehicles. Leads a comfortable life. Stamina goes down because of women if Moon is in Vrischika rashi.	Loses wealth because of women. May be imprisoned because of them.	Lacks courage. Blessed with wealth, properties, conveyances, jewellery and damsels.	Active but not attractive. Attached to other people's wives. Lacks luxuries.
Vrishaba / Tula	Wealthy, learned, diplomatic, elegant body. Owns properties, jewellery and vehicles. Enjoys the pleasures of the bed.	Military commander or a minister. Favourite of the monarch. Renowned. Leads a comfortable life.	Attractive and delicate body. Wealthy. Fashionable. Loves the pleasures of the bed. Gets ornaments of others.	Favourite of the king. High levels of stamina. Loves the pleasures of food, wine and women. Wealthy.

Mithuna / Kanya	Blessed with best wife (May have more than one if Mercury in Kanya). Wealthy and leads a luxurious life. Owns jewellery, properties and conveyances.	Attractive. Prosperous. Enjoys good food and clothing. Works under women.	Attractive to women. Enjoys conjugal happiness. Luxurious life. Works for benefit of religious places.	Maybe a yoga master. Artistic. May run an art shop for women.
Kataka	Good-looking. Blessed with wealth and gold. Fashionable. Enjoys the company and gets the benefit of damsels.	Suffers on account of women. He is insulted and loses money.	Many wives. Rich and possess jewels and luxury items. Attractive. Happy in life.	Scion of a royal family. Lacks pleasures and good looks. Devoid of comforts. Unhappy.
Simha	Wealthy. Loves the company of women. May work under them. Learned. Keeps poor health.	Enjoys the company of several women. Leads a luxurious life. Cheerful and youthful.	Good-looking. Favourite of the ladies. Honoured by the king. High levels of stamina.	Good-looking. Women are inimical to him. Slow progress but wealthy and happy as he ages.
Dhanu / Meena	Blessed with good wife and sons. Wealthy. Sweet-tempered. Good-looking. Amorous.	Generous. Possess jewellery and rare forms of art. Rich. Attractive. Enjoys the pleasures of the bed.	Attractive. Intelligent, learned and wealthy. Happy in life. Fortunate and long-lived.	Maybe an adopted child or have foster parents. Loves to work. Travels a lot. Loves nature.

Makara / Kumbha	Wealthy. Has affairs with other people's wives. Suffers on account of his sons. Sinful and seldom happy. Lacks courage and friends.	Luxurious. Gets benefits from damsels. Quarrelsome.	Wealthy and owns properties, jewellery, vehicles. Gets the comfort of women. Enjoys food, wine and damsels.	Good-looking and wealthy. Happy and enjoys the pleasures he gets. Attached to other people's wives.

Example 21:

Jupiter (R)	Moon	Rahu	
	Asc Saturn Ketu	Sun Mars (C) Mercury (R)	Venus

The above birth chart is that of a renowned politician of India who served as the country's deputy prime minister. Although the lagna is not well placed, the mutual aspect between Venus and Jupiter has meant that the politician has had a long and successful career in his chosen profession and has been blessed with a good family life. Intelligent and scholarly, he is famous for his political and organizational skills and is long-lived. Saturn's influence on the lagna has meant that all good things came to him late in life after much effort on his part.

Aspects of Saturn:

Saturn is the most dreaded and feared planet among the navagrahas by many who believe in astrology. This is because, Saturn is a hard taskmaster who believes in discipline, patience, perseverance and hard work. People will feel, its job is to restrict, delay, inhibit and restrict their desires. In reality, Saturn is the planet that can give the maximum amount of rewards but it wants the native to puts in tons of effort to reap the fruits of his labour. Basically, Saturn doesn't like any short cuts which is why many have suffered at the hands of Saturn because of their bad karma. It is a slow moving, cold and calculating planet driven heavily by karma that changes its sign once in 2.5 years. It is a planet of the asuras.

Naturally, Saturn will try and transfer these qualities on the planet and house it is aspecting in any rashi chart. Saturn's aspect on its enemy planets of Sun, Moon and Mars can be much more severe and can inhibit the native's personality and character development as well as their intellect.

Jupiter, in addition to the 7th house aspect, also fully aspects (100% aspect) the 3rd and 10th house from where it sits. As always, one must take into account the houses and signs Saturn owns, the house and sign that it is placed in along with its dignity in the shadbala table and apply the same principle on the planet it aspects. Saturn, like Jupiter and Mars, may aspect another planet without it being aspected by that very same planet. Likewise, Jupiter and Mars may aspect Saturn without Saturn aspecting them. Saturn's negative aspect on another planet (eg: Sun or Moon) may be nullified by a large extent if Jupiter is aspecting Saturn without Saturn in turn aspecting Jupiter. Instead of Jupiter, if it is Mars, then the negative forces only grow.

For example, if Saturn placed in Dhanu rashi is aspecting Moon, its negative influence can be reduced if Jupiter placed in Simha rashi is aspecting Saturn. Instead, if Mars is aspecting Saturn then then the negative influence only grows.

Table No. 37: Aspects of Saturn on various planets placed in:

Part A:

	Sun	Moon	Mars	Mercury
Mesha / Vrischika	Lacks Intelligence. Keeps poor health. Careless in work.	Comes from lower family. Disliked by others. Inimical by nature. Uncouth and poor conduct. Dishonest. Devoid of wealth.	Courageous in actions. Poor speech. Lacks stamina. Attached to others wives.	Sorrowful. Fierce and loves to crush enemies. Lacks friends and relations.
Vrishaba / Tula	Lazy, indolent, poor-conduct, ill-tempered. Suffers from chronic disease. Attached to older women.	Lacks happiness. Damsels are against him. Problems for mother's or father's health. Better for wealth for Moon in Tula but not for Moon in Vrishaba. Loves sex.	Happy, renowned and wealthy. Head of village or town. Good relations and friends.	Unhappy. Losses because of relations. Uncouth appearance. Faces calamities.
Mithuna / Kanya	Many servants. Agitated mind. Engaged in supporting a number of relations. Cunning.	Devoid of wealth. Women take away his money and have a negative influence on him. Unhappy. Poor memory. Problem for mother.	May do work related to agriculture, mines, forts or forests. Poor and sorrowful. Uncouth appearance.	Rises steadily in life. Efforts lead to success. Courteous. Luxurious life.

Kataka	Crooked mind. Back-biter. Suffers from diseases arising out of wind or water.	Unhappy. Wanderer. Poor. Dishonest. Sinful. Of low character.	Gains money through water related professions. Elegant body. Actions equal to a prince.	Hypocrite. Sinful. Devoid of good qualities. Faces imprisonment. Poor relation with siblings and gurus.
Simha	Sabotages other people's efforts and is successful. Causes distress to others. Impotent.	Lacks wealth. Connected to agri profession. Unhappy. Lacks female companion. Mean minded, dishonest. Works as a guard.	Looks old. Lives in rented places. Lacks wealth. Wanderer. Sorrowful.	Dry and large body. Perspires a lot in life. Lacks comforts. Sorrowful. Not good-looking.
Dhanu / Meena	Untidy. Maintains himself at others cost. Attached to low people. Loves animal related sports.	Better for Dhanu rashi. Native is sweet, well bred, gentle and learned. For Moon in Meena, native becomes restless, lacks intelligence, wife and sons.	Lacks a good body. Fond of strife and battle. Wanderer. Unhappy. Sinful.	Loves mountains, forests and nature. Traveller. Glutton. Slovenly appearance. His objectives lead to frustration.
Makara / Kumbha	Easily destroys his enemies. Prosperous. Favourite of the monarch.	Rich but uncouth and slovenly in appearance. Attached to others wives. Lazy and indolent.	Intelligent, learned, courageous. Rich and powerful. Lucky with children but unlucky with women.	Sinful. Hard-working. Poor. Humble and sorrowful.

Part B:

	Jupiter	Venus
Mesha / Vrischika	Courageous, greedy and lazy. Sharp in temper. Gets praised by one and all. Has fickle minded friends.	Lethargic, Wanders aimlessly. Thievish tendencies. Works under someone of similar temperament.
Vrishaba / Tula	Intelligent, learned. Wealthy. Head of a village or town. Unattractive, lazy. Lacks conjugal bliss.	Lacks wealth. Unhappy. Ill-tempered. Chronic disease. Wife of lower strata.
Mithuna / Kanya	Attractive. Head of a state, town or village.	Defeated by enemies. Fickle, inimical and stupid. Leads a life of grief.
Kataka	Occupies a high position. Talkative. Accumulates wealth steadily.	Fickle, poor and fallen. Unattractive. Unhappy. Under influence of wife.
Simha	Gets the benefit of many damsels. Sweet-talker. Eloquent. Unhappy. Artistic. May choose such a profession.	Occupies a very high position. Wealthy and propertied. Attached to widows. Attractive but sorrowful.
Dhanu / Meena	Attractive. Lazy. Poor and humble. Heckled by others. Unhappy. Irreligious.	Attractive. Wealthy, happy and commands many luxuries. Happy and comfortable life.
Makara / Kumbha	Owns cattle and has number of servants. Learned. Wealthy. Occupies a pre-eminent position. Enjoys life.	Wealthy and has a number of conveyances. Dark but attractive personality. Lazy and untidy.

Example 22:

Moon			Ketu
			Jupiter
Mars			
Rahu	Venus (R)	Asc Sun Mercury (R) Saturn (C)	

Example 22 shows the birth chart of a celebrity from the world of cinema. He has had one of the most successful innings as a movie personality in modern day India and has ventured into politics. Note the 10th house aspect of Saturn on Jupiter has blessed him longevity rarely seen in any profession in his chosen field. In addition to his acting skills, he has donned the role of a director, producer, singer and composer and has even written dialogues for his movies. He continues to occupy a high position, be in the limelight and is wealthy.

Chapter 6

Karma and Astrology

I have always been a great believer in the concept of Karma. While Vedic Astrology is an ancient science which is still being studied across the world as people try to understand its purity and precision, many assumptions related to this science have scope for lots of improvement, which is why predictions made by people with half-baked knowledge of the subject often go wrong.

Vedic Astrology is a science of tendencies and takes an individual or any other entity along a certain path. It does not guarantee the occurrence of a particular event. Think of a Cricket match between two teams A and B. If A is a world champion side while B is a novice in the sport, we can say with very high levels of confidence that A is likely to win the match. This is the most likely outcome based on past history of the two teams. This is however not a guarantee that A will win the match. Other factors such as the performance of the two sides on the day, weather conditions (Possibility of rain?) will all have to be taken into account. Historical studies have shown that the science of Vedic astrology is known to have near perfect levels of accuracy when the assumptions that have been taken into account are correct. An astrologer making a prediction about his client's future could go wrong if he uses a Panchang (Almanac) that has an Ayanamsa which is so different, that the client's rashi chart shows an incorrect ascendant or Lagna. Remember, if the assumptions made with respect to a data are incorrect, then the analysis and the resulting forecasts are bound to go wrong.

This brings me to the point on Karma. Karma is nothing but simply our actions which will produce a set of results either in line or outside of our expectations. As you sow, so shall you reap. This old adage which is often used in our lives is particularly true in the case of predictive science like astrology. If a swamiji tells an average student with a poor track record in Mathematics that he is going to score 100% in the subsequent maths exam no matter what, that still doesn't give the student the right to not prepare for the exam and believe that 100% is assured. It would be foolish on the part of the student to take a lackadaisical approach believing that 100% is written for him in his destiny.

Human beings are given the opportunity to write their own destiny on planet Earth. Remember, that in a battle between fate and free-will, the latter has the ability to overcome the former through sheer will power and hard work. Planets of course are there to act as a guiding force. A young student who has a flair and passion for music and singing as well as for Cricket and is unable to make up his mind on which of his talents to pursue as a career will of course have a number of mentors, advisers and well-wishers to guide him through his nascent years. Astrology can come in handy in such situations and point to how life might progress for this individual when he pursues either of his two talents as a vocation. In fact astrology will be able to tell us what direction or shape his life will take but it is up to the individual to make these predictions come true through his karma. For example, it can be clearly seen in the birth charts of Lata Mangeshkar and Sachin Tendulkar why they chose playback singing in the film industry and Cricket as their respective professions. Imagine what would have happened not only to them but also to Bollywood and Cricket had it been the other way around?

Concept 1: The Curious case of Rahu and Jupiter (Guru)

A lot has been discussed in several books and blogs on planetary friendships and enmities. Like humans, planets also exhibit a number of characteristics and are known for their own set of inherent qualities.

Among the navargrahas, the planets of Rahu are Guru (Jupiter) are one set of polar opposites. Rahu is the planet of asuras while Jupiter is the planet of the devas. Rahu is considered to be a malefic planet while Jupiter is the best benefic among the navagrahas. Jupiter is masculine while Rahu is feminine. Rahu's element is air while Jupiter's element is ether or space. Jupiter is Saatvik in nature while Rahu is Taamsik. Thus Rahu and Jupiter differ like chalk and cheese in all their gunas.

Jupiter is a benevolent planet that likes to take the correct path in life. It is known for its depth and methodical and steady approach. It gives its rewards after much effort.

While Rahu on the other hand, is a planet of suddenness which can make a beggar a king overnight or vice-versa. It loves speculation, gambling and shortcuts. Rewards with Rahu are sudden.

Such difference in their nature, perception and tastes make Rahu and Jupiter 'A' grade enemies. Wherever Jupiter shines, Rahu goes quiet and likewise, Rahu's glory can make Jupiter feel weak.

It can seldom be seen in any rashi chart of the native based on their lagna or ascendant that both Rahu and Jupiter can work well for the native. Usually one of these planets is strong for the native while the other is weak.

In the Vimshottari Dasha system of Vedic astrology, the mahadasha of Rahu which lasts for 18 years is followed by the mahadasha of Jupiter which covers a span of 16 years. The transition from mahadasha of Rahu to the mahadasha of Jupiter is a much talked about one. If Rahu and Jupiter are placed in neighbouring signs or 2-12 position in a birth chart (eg: Rahu in Tula and Jupiter in Kanya), it is termed as the Dwidwadasha dosha. The relative placement of Rahu and Jupiter in 6th or 8th sign (6-8 position) from each other in a birth chart (eg: Rahu in Mesha and Jupiter in Kanya) is termed as the Sashtashtaga dosha.

Such relative placements of Rahu and Jupiter creates complications and turmoil during the transition from Rahu mahadasha to Jupiter mahadasha. Specifically, the last 6 months of Rahu mahadasha and the first 6 months of Jupiter mahadasha can be challenging and tricky. This period is known as the Dasa Sandhi period.

Finally, Rahu being the planet of suddenness, gambling and thievery, if well placed can take an individual to extraordinary heights during its mahadasha even if the native indulged in sinful acts or dubious practices. This type of fame and acclaim however would not be everlasting and is likely to come crashing down during the dasa sandhi period between Rahu and Jupiter particularly if Rahu and Jupiter are 2-12 or 6-8 position.

Numerous studies have shown that any sudden rise in a native's life during initial years of Rahu mahadahsa (The planet of hallucination and maya) which is driven by blind luck will not last and either by the end of the Rahu mahadahsa or beginning of Jupiter mahadasha the native will lose everything that he had gained during the Rahu period.

Example 23:

			Rahu
Ketu			Moon
Jupiter	Venus	Asc Mercury (C) Saturn	Sun Mars (C)

Example 23 shows the birth chart of a former Prime Minister of her country. She was known for her uncompromising politics and leadership style which earned her the nickname the "Iron Lady". Her ascendant, Tula, has Saturn placed in it. Saturn of course here is exalted and gives rise to the pancha mahapurusha yoga known as Sasa Maha yoga. This makes the native a born leader of men and women who holds a very high office of influence in the native's country or a position of repute in the planet. The main phase of the native's professional career was during the mahadasha of Rahu between September 1972 and September 1990. She became leader of opposition during the period of Rahu-Rahu and rose to the office of the Prime Minister in 1979 during the period of Rahu-Saturn. Her reign resulted in a remarkable transformation of her country's economy as she led the implementation of the concept of privatization of national companies thereby boosting the productivity and growth in the economy and bringing out of doldrums. She served as the Prime Minister for 11 years till 1990 when challenges to her leadership from her own party resulted in her stepping down from the office of the PM in November 1990. She had become very individualistic towards the end of her premiership and started taking decisions which was not in line with either her earlier ideologies or proclivities which resulted in her and her party's popularity drastically falling.

Rahu placed in the 10th house of profession gave her a spectacular rise in the field of politics and took her right to the top during its mahadasha. This was the best period of her life and she remained in the limelight for the entire span of 18 years of this mahadasha. But as soon as the mahadasha of Jupiter started, her career was over. Jupiter is placed in its own rashi but is a functional malefic for Tula lagna natives as it owns the 3rd and 6th houses. Indeed, the opposition and enmity from her own party resulted in her losing her office. Note how Rahu and Jupiter are placed in 6-8 position relative to each other. The dasa-sandhi period of Rahu and Jupiter was the trigger for her downfall.

Example 24:

	Sun Venus (C) Mercury Ketu	Mars	
			Jupiter (R)
Moon	Saturn (R)	Asc Rahu	

The birth chart shown in example 24 is that of a highly renowned and famous businessman. Native was born at the cusp of Tula lagna and Vrishcika lagna. Lagna lord Venus is placed in the 7th house while 3rd house of courage has Moon placed in it and its owner Jupiter is placed in the 11th house of gains. This indicates the native gains through the risks he takes in his business. Moon's ownership of the 10th house indicates, the native's profession will have connections with water. He may himself reside close to a large water body. The start of Rahu mahadasha in 2001 saw the death of his father which was followed by a dispute with his brother where the native claimed most of the businesses built by his father. The native is known for his aggressive business dealings where he is also known to indulge in ruthless and sometimes questionable practices. His business empire expanded through the Rahu mahadasha where he diversified into other new businesses. The start of the Jupiter mahadasha in late 2019 which is placed in the 11th house of gains has seen him monetise two of his businesses with his wealth multiplying manifold. This author however feels that Jupiter's ownership of 2 dushtasthana houses (3rd and 6th) will lead to a number of problems particularly with regards to his health (6th indicates diseases, debts and enemies) and he is unlikely to ever see the heights in his business that he enjoyed during the mahadasha of Rahu. There may be some liver related ailment (Jupiter governs fat related organs) which might be difficult for him to cure. Placement of 5th owner Saturn in the 2nd house (Saturn is also retrograde) may also lead to inheritance related disputes with regards to his business empire as far as the next generation is concerned.

Example 25:

	Sun Mercury (C) Venus (R) Mars		Rahu
			Saturn
Jupiter Moon Ketu			Asc

The above chart is that of a world famous leader and dictator of the 20th century. This native was known for his authoritarian style of functioning and didn't hesitate to indulge in open warfare and conflict if the situation led him along that path. He was one of the central figures in the Second World War. Born in Kanya lagna, the native had lagna lord in the 8th house of disputes and sudden occurrences. He rose to the position of Chancellor of his country in 1933 during the period of Rahu mahadasha Rahu antardasha. Rahu's period which started in 1931 turned out to be the defining moment for him, his country and the world at large during the first half of the century. Placed in the 10th house, it gave him a sudden rise in his country's politics and took him to the top of his chosen profession but his dubious approach led him along a path of destruction and during the period of Rahu-Venus in 1945, he ended his own life after losing the war. Venus owning the 2nd house is one of the maraka planets in his horoscope and sits with three other planets in the 8th house which is a dushtasthana. This is another classic case of Rahu elevating an individual to the top and then completely either ending his career or life.

While it is believed by many that a spectacular rise during the period of Rahu mahadasha, especially from the beginning of this 18 year period, aided by blind luck can take the native to the top and then drop him to rock bottom minimum, it is also accepted by many that a breakthrough during the final years of the Rahu mahadasha aided by plenty of hard work will make the native continue to rise in his profession during the subsequent mahadasha of Jupiter, provided the blessing of Jupiter is present in the horoscope.

This can be seen by the chart in Example 20, where the native began his career during the final years of Rahu period and rose to the top of his craft during the period of Jupiter.

Concept 2: Why Ketu is feared the most?

Ketu is the most feared among the navagrahas by many practitioners of Vedic Astrology. Although public perception suggests that Saturn or Shani is the most difficult and tedious among the 9 planets, it is the mahadasha (or antardasha) of Ketu that astrologers talk about the most.

Ketu, like Rahu, is a planet of the asuras and is malefic by nature. It is a taamsik feminine planet. Like Rahu, it is a planet of sudden occurrences and speculation. Both are shadow planets. However, the similarity between the two ends there.

Rahu is considered to be a planet that makes the beggar a king overnight. It can provide very high levels of materialistic success and fame. It is a planet of gambling, thievery, poison, alcohol, debauched individuals etc. Ketu, on the other hand, is the planet of spirituality and salvation. It is also known as moksha-karaka. It can bestow wisdom, powers of discrimination and spiritual knowledge. It gives one psychic abilities.

For a materialistically minded person, these qualities can turn out to be very damaging, much more so than Saturn and Rahu. Ketu signifies loss, liberation, perception, wisdom, lack of confidence, negation, self-doubt, fantasies, drug addiction, alcoholism, injury, spiritual insight.

In a nutshell, Ketu denies what any normal human being craves. Materialistic success, wealth, name, fame, conjugal happiness, properties and conveyances. Ketu, like Jupiter, can provide spiritual advancement but unlike Jupiter, does not bestow wealth and happiness.

There have been many instances where the mahadasha of Ketu has resulted in the native's life spinning out of control so much that he or she has contemplated ending their life. Of course, in most of these cases they have been unable to do so resulting in them seeing hell on earth.

The ruling deity of Ketu is Lord Ganesha who is the chief patron of all forms of arts and sciences, lord of all good beginnings, bestower of wisdom, success and wealth, spiritual and materialistic knowledge and success, and the chief remover of all obstacles in life. Constant prayer to Lord Vinayaka for his spiritual blessing goes a long way in alleviating the negative effects of Ketu.

Example 26:

			Jupiter Mercury Ketu
			Sun Moon (C)
			Venus
Rahu Mars (R)		Saturn	Asc

Example 26 shows the horoscope of a stock broker who rose to such heights during his prime time that his popularity rivalled that of any politician, cinema star or even a world famous sportsperson. Lagna lord Mercury is placed in the 10th house of profession in his own house. This gives rise to the panchamahapurusha yoga called Bhadra yoga. Bhadra yoga natives are blessed with high levels of intelligence, wit, humor, fast and sweet talking ability, and communication skills akin to that of a world leader as well as language and mathematical ability. It is one of the best yogas to have for a successful businessman or trader. The main mahadasha in this native's life was Mercury mahadasha which ran from 1973 to 1990 which completely changed not only changed his and his family's life, but also that of the equity trading culture in his country. Coming from a humble background, this native started out by doing odd jobs. He began his career in the financial services industry by taking a position as a jobber at a stock exchange around 1980 and finally starting his own brokerage firm. His approach which was very novel and refreshing, resulted in him becoming a highly successful and ultra-wealthy man owning properties and a fleet of branded and imported vehicles and earned him the nickname the “Big Bull”. He had his legion of fans who swore by his name. However all this changed when the mahadasha of Ketu started in late 1990. Attracting the envy of his rivals in the trading industry as well as that of the powers that be, he was arrested on account of securities fraud and stock market manipulation that he had indulged in and numerous charges were filed against him. He was ultimately released from jail but was banned from trading and investing in the stock market. He tried to make a brief comeback as a trading guru but was arrested once again as the mahadasha of Venus began. Venus is placed in the 12th house of losses and during the period of Venus-Sun in 2001 he died of a heart attack.

This of course is an example of how an individual who was riding on the crest of wave, suffered indignity and humiliation during the main period of Ketu which ultimately cost him his life.

The above examples in this chapter show, how planets function according to our karma and ultimately give us the results we deserved. In example 20, the individual toiled hard during the mahadasha of Rahu and got the fruits of his labour during the mahadasha of Jupiter but in examples 23, 25 and 26, we saw how an individual trying to subvert or game the system faced humiliation and perennial fall from grace.

Conclusion:

Planets like human beings are entities with their own set of qualities. Remember, we reside in one such entity called the Earth. They act as a guiding force for us. If understood and interpreted in the right manner, they can work wonders for any individual and bless him or her with spiritual and material happiness according to his qualities and karma.

About the Author

Srinivasan Gopalan is a Computer Science Engineer by training and an Investment and Finance professional. Vedic Astrology which started as a hobby has turned into a serious passion and Srinivasan has constantly been researching this ancient science and the implications it has on our everyday lives. His areas of interest include dasha systems, mundane astrology and the divisional charts. In his second book on Vedic astrology, Srinivasan delves into the scientific principles behind the concepts of retrogression, combustion, conjunction and aspects among the planets and fortifies his arguments with real life examples to allow for a faster and more intuitive way of learning the subject.